little white ^marketing lies

The Misconceptions Blocking Your Business Success

from the author of
365 Days of Marketing

Elizabeth Kraus

Owner/CEO, Be InPulse Branding Marketing & Design

www.12monthsofmarketing.com

I0473871

Little White Marketing Lies

by Elizabeth Kraus

Owner/CEO, Be InPulse Branding Marketing & Design

www.12monthsofmarketing.com

Author/Editor: Elizabeth Kraus
Cover and Interior Design/Lay out: Elizabeth Kraus (Be InPulse Branding, Marketing & Design)

Printing History: 2012 First Edition

ISBN 9781470118778

To my parents, Jim and Sheryll Robinson
who always made me believe that everything is possible,
and always taught me to face things as they are.

To my children, Amanda and Gavon, Eric and Laura,
Sarah, Sam, Noa and Rania
and to my grandchildren, Jaxon and Jaycee
whose possibilities are endless.

To my husband, Dan
who brought my heart back to life, makes me laugh
and makes sure I believe in myself.

Elizabeth

"If you are out to describe the truth,
leave elegance to the tailor."

Albert Einstein

little white ^marketing lies

The Misconceptions Blocking
Your Business Success

Introduction

Bad leadership can never produce happy employees. Unhappy employees can never produce satisfied customers. And unsatisfied customers will never produce sales and referrals. Everything starts at the top.

When your business is not doing well or you are not getting the results you expected it's normal to look in all directions hoping to find a cause, preferably one that you can control or change.

I cannot explain why this is true, but I think too often we assume that it must be something outside of our business that is keeping us from success, and so it's there that we look first. It's tempting to shift the blame outward in many directions, such as:

- the slow economy
- your competitors
- lack of consumer education (if they only knew how great our product was, they would buy it)
- lack of engagement and buy in from employees
- our own customers, resenting them for not being loyal to our business as a result of all we've "done for them" or (worse) how awesome we are

I have news for you and it's something that you might not want to hear: If you are not getting the results that you want or your business is not doing particularly well, you are probably NOT awesome.

"Facts do not cease to exist because they are ignored."

Aldous Huxley (1894–1963) English writer

The truth is, the first place you should look when things are not going right and the first problems you need to solve to change things are much, much closer to home. Closer even than your own employees, because the first problems you need to solve are those that you can only discover when looking directly into the mirror.

Every problem in your organization, in one way or another, can be traced back to ground zero, and that is leadership. Because as the leader of your organization, everything about your organization begins with you.

Slow economy? It's an excuse; because you can point to other businesses just like yours who are doing better.

The competition? If you are being outwitted, outrun and outmaneuvered by direct and indirect competitors then you may be approaching things from the wrong angle. Either way, it's not their awesomeness, it's your lack of awesomeness that is holding you back.

Do you believe that what your company provides and the way in which you provide it is superior to the competition, and should therefore be helping you win that battle? If not, why should your customers? Presuming you do believe that, why don't your customers and prospects believe it to be true?

Lack of consumer education? At what point will you be forced to acknowledge that your prospects and customers have been educated, and still don't want what you have? And if they are not buying what you have, or are choosing other products or businesses over yours, we are back to an internal problem. You have failed to identify the real need of the prospect or customer. You have failed to provide the right product or you are doing it poorly.

Lack of employee engagement? Now we are getting closer. If you ascribe to the little white marketing lie that your employees are paid to care—that employee engagement is something exchanged for paychecks—you are sorely mistaken.

There are a whole lot of reasons that your employees might not choose to identify themselves with the brand of your business, why they might not be engaged and inspired enough to help you solve problems or provide exceptional, extraordinary service to your customers, or why they might not even want to refer their own friends and family to your business. And all trails lead straight back to you as the leader of your business and the culture that you have created (or failed to create) within your business.

Lack of customer loyalty? Bingo—the end of the food chain. Your customers are not loyal, nor are they appreciative enough to come back. They are not excited enough to tell other people about you. They don't want more of what you have to offer. You can try to blame them for being greedy, price driven or ignorant, you can condescendingly shake your head, tsk tsk-ing at their lack of wisdom.

Or you can take a look squarely in the mirror and admit that bad leadership can never produce happy employees. Unhappy employees can never produce satisfied customers. And unsatisfied customers will never produce sales and referrals. Everything starts at the top.

No matter what external forces you try to overcome, without a sound center—an authentically good culture at the core of your business, led by people who share these values in theory and in practice—without that solid foundation you simply cannot build the kind of business you claim you want to have.

You will not be able to attract the right kind of people to your staff and you will not be able to inspire and engage your employees to feats of awesomeness.

And without awesomeness, you cannot hope to retain, engage and motivate customers to take the actions you want them to take.

If you have been ignoring the facts when it comes to the culture and values of your business, there is no time like the present acknowledge them and begin to take the steps you need to take to rebuild your business the right way. The only thing worse than ignoring the facts, is to ignore the facts for one more day. It's going to be a great year!

So what are "Little White Marketing Lies," anyway?

Little white marketing lies are falsities we tell people (and sometimes even tell ourselves) that we believe to be benign, harmless.

And there are little white marketing lies we tell all the time that are keeping our businesses from success.

Little White Marketing Lie #1:

"We provide exceptional customer service."

It's a lie when you say it, it's a lie when just about any business owner says it.

Why?

Because of exactly that: *everyone* says it.

When I ask a business owner what's so special about their business, it's first thing that they tell me. *Every* time.

Obviously, it cannot be true of every business, and if it is true of most businesses, it's still not true.

Because by definition, in order to be extraordinary requires for something to be unusual, remarkable or surprising and outside of the established order.

By definition, if *everyone* is "exceptional," then *no one* is.

The real question is, what *about* your customer service is surprising or remarkable—so extraordinary, if you will—that clients walk out the door and are compelled to tell other people about it?

If you cannot pinpoint **how** the customer service your business provides, day in and day out, is truly outside of what they expect, then it's probably not exceptional.

I would argue that most of what occurs in the vast majority of businesses merely falls within customer expectations.

> Your customers expect to be treated like guests.
>
> Your customers expect to receive a great service or buy a product that does what was promised.
>
> Your customers expect for you and your employees to be cheerful and helpful.
>
> Your customers expect you to be extra-knowledgeable and able to provide expertise and advice for them in areas related to your business, industry, products, new techniques and trends.

So even if you do all these things, you are doing no more than meeting your client's basic expectations.

And there is *nothing exceptional* about *meeting* expectations.

What's more, even when it comes to meeting customer expectations, many business owners are lying to themselves.

Take the results of a 2011 Global Customer Satisfaction Barometer, conducted by American Express*. According to the study:

> 70% of Americans said they would be willing to spend almost 15% more with businesses they believed (really) provided excellent customer service.

With such an indicator, you would think that businesses would make customer service a top priority; but in the same survey:

> 60% of respondents said they don't believe businesses are making customer service a high priority.

> In fact, 26% said they think businesses are actually paying *less* attention to service. Only 29% of US consumers said that recent shopping experiences exceeded their expectations.

> Only 24% of US consumers believe that you value their business and will go the extra mile to keep it.

> 48% of those who said they would not pay more for good service said it's because they expect good service, every time. *(And why shouldn't they?)*

Why is there such a vast difference between what most business owners claim to be true about their businesses and what their customers are saying?

The disconnect seems to be in the way that "excellent (or exceptional, or extraordinary or whatever other superlative you are claiming) customer service" is defined.

Most business owners who claim to be providing extra-ordinary customer service are really just meeting basic expectations. They believe they provide an extraordinary experience, but, as the statistics demonstrate, only one out of every four of their customers agree that they are going beyond the call of duty.

Guess what; that is exactly why customers are not telling their friends and family about your business, and that is one of the main reasons why your books are not full and your retail shelves are.

[*]SOURCE: http://about.americanexpress.com/news/docs/2011x/AXP_2011_csbar_market.pdf

Customer service is *not* contained in the actions of a person taking or fulfilling an order, receiving a return or complaint, performing a service or selling a product.

Customer service is not an action; rather it's a process— an intentionally designed system—meant to enhance the customer's experience and which influences whether a customer *feels* satisfied or dissatisfied by a product or service.

Did you catch that?

It's not about whether you did everything exactly right during the course of an interaction with a customer. It's about how they *felt* when they walked away from the experience.

You can do everything perfectly, quickly, cheerfully and helpfully; but if the customer doesn't *feel* something special when they do business with you, then you have *not* provided them with exceptional customer service.

Something about the customer experience has to be *outside* of what they expect to occur. It has to be more and different than they expected, in a positive way.

It's not just about making the customer experience "better." It's about making it greater in value, bigger and/or more sophisticated—more than that of the competition and more than the customer expects—so that it stands out to the customer as inherently and uniquely extra-ordinary.

To do that, you have to truly understand your customers—you have to go beyond trying to guess what they **might** want and find out what they really do want, what they truly value, and what makes them feel valued and special.

And then you must train, educate and empower employees to respond to requests, complaints, unique situations and individual customer's needs and desires in ways that speak to those values.

And on top of all that, you have to build the unexpected into client experiences. Your customer's experience must in some way be outside of the normal, expected order of things.

Is there *anything* about the experience you provide for your customers that would be surprising and outside of the expected order of things when compared to their treatment by competitors or other businesses?

If you are stuck here, scratching your head about how to do this, maybe that is a good thing.

If it were easy and obvious, everyone would be doing it.

But the fact is, few businesses are serving their customers in an exceptional way, so the field is wide open for you.

- Do market research.

- Survey and solicit feedback from your customers.

- Form a customer focus group.

- Do secret shopping.

- Brainstorm with your employees.

- Analyze each customer touch point from a purely customer-centric point of view.

If you wonder why people don't always agree with the claim you make that your business provides "exceptional customer service" or why the customer experience at your business is not helping you gain and retain clients, it's likely that what you have in place is not actually enough to influence the customer to feel exceptionally satisfied!

More?

Let's talk about how you can really pamper your clients (and why that would be a good thing):

> **pam-per-ing** (*verb, means to*)
> indulge with every attention, comfort, and kindness;
> spoil;
> the act of indulging or gratifying a *desire*;
> gratifying *tastes, appetites,* or *desires*
> (http://thefreedictionary.com/pampering)

Have you ever had someone try to make you happy, not with what you really wanted, needed or desired and not in a way that you value, but who tried to make you happy by giving you what they believed you should want?

In other words, they did not really want to make you happy— they wanted you to be happy with what they want you to be happy with. They wanted you to be happy with what they wanted to give you, whether or not it gratified your tastes, appetites or desires.

They sort of wanted you to be happy, but did not do the work to find out what would really make you happy.

I have.

I was in a long term relationship with a man who did not care what I really needed or wanted from the relationship. He tried to keep me in the relationship by giving me things he thought I might like, rather than working to improve the relationship. He mistakenly thought that things and money (or the threat of losing things or money) would be inducements strong keep me in the relationship—a relationship that was not meeting my needs, let alone gratifying my desires. A relationship that, as it stood, was not meeting my needs in the present and could not meet my needs in the future.

I think that there is a parallel to be made to the relationship you have with your customers, and to the idea of creating a customer experience that leaves your customers feeling understood and pampered—indulged with what matters most *to them*—what gratifies *their* tastes, appetites and desires.

By definition, in order to pamper your customers you have to have a real handle on *their* true needs and wants. If you try to guess what your customers want or give them what you would want (if you were them) then you could be missing the mark by a wide margin.

What's more, if people feel that you are trying to coerce or mislead them through some form of bribery to remain in a relationship with your business, it could lead to a loss of trust, loss of customer confidence, and to the loss of customers themselves.

"In business, you get what you want by giving other people what they want."

(Alice MacDougall)

So how can you know what your customers want? Here are 10 places to start to find out what your customers really want, so that you can spoil them!

1. Ask customers what they want in surveys at the point of sale or to follow up after appointments or purchases by e-mail.

2. Create a formal customer (and/or employee) suggestion system. Respond to each and every entry, even if it is only to acknowledge that you heard the request and will keep it in mind for the future.

   If and when you implement changes based on customer requests, publicize this in your e-mail newsletter, direct mailings to customers, and/or in signage noting which new products, services or process improvements were added specifically because of customer requests.

   This will send all of your customers a strong message about how important what they want is to you and your team. And it can also result in additional comments and suggestions that lead to more improvements.

   As James Cash Penney (founder of J.C. Penney) once said, "Change is vital; **improvement** is the logical form of change."

3. Add a product or service request form to your website.

4. Poll your employees (especially those employees who have the most contact with your customers).

5. Implement an incentive program to reward employees or even customers who make suggestions that result in improvements to the customer experience.

6. Network with peers — even competitors — to share ideas, discuss common customer complaints or requests and brainstorm solutions, and to share ideas which lead to improvements in the customer experience.

7. Respond to each and every customer complaint. Acknowledge the individual and their feelings. If you made a mistake, apologize, and do what you can to make it right. Be transparent.

8. Be available. Spend time interacting personally with your best customers (or with all customers).

9. Make personal contacts with your most valuable customers throughout the year to gauge satisfaction and to ask "What could we do better?"

10. Communicate with your customers on a variety of channels that provide for two-way communication and feedback.

    From old-school community bulletin boards to e-mail newsletters, a blog site, Facebook, Twitter and other social media, it's never been so easy to converse with your customers and prospects.

    Engage in two-way dialogue, ask provoking questions, hold contests, and solicit feedback — whether negative or positive — and monitor and respond to public feedback.

What love can teach you about marketing

This quote tells you what can love can teach you about marketing—branding—your business:

"Love is just a word
until someone comes along
and gives it meaning."

Throughout our lives, love is defined for us by the individuals closest to us: parents, grandparents, aunts and uncles, early childhood caregivers and teachers, sisters and brothers and cousins—and then as we grow older, friends, boyfriends or girlfriends, fiancés and other significant others, and ultimately, our spouses and children.

When you think about the word "love," everything that comes to mind whether happy or sad, joyful, painful—every memory, every *twitterpated* first date, every heartbreak—every experience and person that has lent meaning to the word becomes part of its definition for you.

And here is what this quote about love should teach you (or remind you) about branding your business:

The name, or brand of your business
are just words until people come along
and give them meaning.

Why? Because the brand of your business is not what you say it is. And it's certainly not your logo or corporate colors. Your brand is made up of all of the meanings given to it by your customers, your prospects, your friends, your family—anyone who comes into contact with any aspect of your business.

All of these people assign emotional meaning to the brand of your business and the name of your business, with each and every point of contact. And every time they hear your business name, or your name, or any of your representative's names (your employees), all of the experiences that have lent meaning to what they believe to be true about your business work together to become the brand of your business in their minds.

You cannot control perceptions. You can, however, work to design and control each and every touch point so that the meanings customers and prospects assign to the brand of your business are likely to be infused with positive perceptions, words and descriptions.

This is what branding is all about: the understanding that every channel by which a prospect or customer comes into contact with you is building the brand of your business in their minds.

And that is also why it is so important to take the time to define what you want those impressions to be, and to design each touch point to consistently represent your desired brand image and messages. That is why it's so important to infuse your business culture with positive, customer-centric values and to hire people who share your values, so that your mission and vision can be fulfilled.

Anything you say about your business is just words, until people assign meaning to the brand of your business. Do you know what meanings your customers and prospects are assigning to your brand, and how to affect them?

Little White Marketing Lie #2:

"Our employees set us apart."

That—as they say—is a distinction without a difference. Why?

Every business enjoys a unique employee culture because no two businesses have exactly the same make-up of people.

(Duh)

Your employees set you apart—so what? So do the employees of *every other* business.

As referenced in Little White Marketing Lie #1: We Provide Exceptional Customer Service, if it's true about *everyone*, it cannot be a valid point of difference for *anyone*.

And just as with the first little white marketing lie, the real question is: just what is so special about your particular blend?

If you want to be able to stand behind the claim that your employees set you apart, you must be able to identify unique capabilities, characteristics, strengths or accomplishments in order to prove it. (And before you try to suggest that what sets your employees apart is their commitment to provision of extraordinary customer service, please re-read the first little white marketing lie!)

If you cannot put your finger on anything *specific*—anything your employees as a group 'do,' provide for customers or infuse into the customer experience that is *different* than the competition and *outside* of customer's expectations—then the claim that your employees set you apart is not a valid unique selling proposition for your business.

That said, if you design and nurture it properly, your employee culture *can* set your business apart from the competition and your employees *can* provide truly exceptional customer experiences.

Here's how:

- **Ground all business policies and practices in core values** with this disclaimer: the values must be authentic to you and shared (or at least supported) by all of the employees in your business.

- Once you have identified (authentic) core values, **build or re-write your policies** around them.

    If you say that the customer is your first priority, then all the polices you have in place should reflect that, and all of your operating practices should be those which promote the utmost in customer convenience, ease of access and satisfaction, from the first point of contact, to the last.

- **Re-write every job description** (including your own). Every responsibility in every job description should tie back in some way to how the task or position supports pursuit of the mission and vision, in ways that are consistent with your core values.

- Ensure that your recruiting and interview process, new hire orientation and training, and continuing training program **for every employee includes**

  (1) telling the story of your business,
  (2) reviewing the mission and vision of the company, and
  (3) discussing the company's core values and how they impact every aspect of your operations.

- Ask employees to **agree (in writing)** to uphold the promises your business makes to customers.

- Encourage innovation and **continuous improvement**. Provide incentives for creative suggestions that help to improve the business. Give employees the incentives and opportunities to try something new, even (and maybe especially) if it is outside of the way you normally do business.

- **Blur the lines.** Don't give employees the impression that because something is technically "not their job" that they are not allowed to provide suggestions, innovate, improve or even take on new responsibilities.

  No employee in your organization (including you) should feel that they have the right to knowingly ignore any problem or shortcoming, especially any problem that can impact the customer relationship.

- **Make it safe** for people to make suggestions or point out shortcomings.

- **Discourage territorial behaviors.**

- **Reward initiative and recognize**—celebrate!—those individuals who most **embody** your core values and seek to **live out** the mission and vision of your business in the course of how they fulfill their role as an employee.

- **Get employee buy-in** when rolling out changes and new initiatives. Be sure every employee knows why changes are necessary or why new initiatives are desirable and the benefits that they can expect as a result (relate the issues so that employees understand how changes and initiatives ultimately benefit *them*: their ability to do their job, customer relations, improved efficiencies, etc., vs. only how they benefit your business).

- **Track, review and report results.**

- **Periodically check in** during long change processes and on-going initiatives to review progress and tweak things where needed. **Get feedback** from employees about whether the benefits you expected to materialize are doing so.

And finally (by the way, this is where you will make or break it) **hold people accountable.**

- **Tie performance reviews and salaries** to employees' demonstration of core values and fulfillment of the mission and vision statement.

- Make sure every employee knows how their role **impacts the customer experience** and how they help to **fulfill the mission and vision** of the organization.

- **Make it safe** for employees to reveal any discrepancies between what you promise customers or your core values, and what is occurring in your operations.

- **Discuss problems** as neutrally as possible—talk about behaviors, not personalities.

- Deal with identified problems **quickly.**

- Deal with people who are missing the mark **privately**.

- **Invest i**n training, retraining and coaching for individuals, but understand that some individuals may not be teachable or coach-able. And,

- **"Believe people when they show you who they are"** (preferably, the first time).

  You are responsible to your customers, to the good of all employees and to your business as a whole, before you are responsible to any one employee.

  Employer loyalty is highly laudable. But employer loyalty is __misplaced__ when it is the cause for retention of an individual who is **damaging** your company from the inside-out, or even actively damaging your client relationships and initiatives.

It's true—you do have a unique blend of employees.

Your employee culture is a reflection of the unique and shared values, beliefs, attitudes, ideas, experiences, assumptions and of the actual behaviors of your staff.

And—for better or for worse—this culture is reflected back to your clients in **every area** of your business and has more ability to influence the success and profitability of your business more than any other.

And the good news is that you have the ability to turn your employee culture into something truly special—something that will be as special to your employees as it is to your customers and your business.

CHAPTER BONUS:

Put meaning back into work

We all know that you spell work using the 4 letters w-o-r-k and we've all heard the phrase, "work is a four letter word," referring to the fact that it's something most of us have to do vs. something that we actually want to do.

But I am going to suggest, instead, that the word "work" is just fine; rather, "job" is my four letter word.

Because a job is something that you do to minimal standards:

- You arrive at your job no later than a certain time

- You leave no earlier than a certain time

- You perform certain tasks or fulfill certain responsibilities

- Or you complete a certain tasks or a certain number of tasks during your shift

Do you see?

"Jobs" are all about simply meeting standard expectations, pursuing "good enough" instead of something more fulfilling.

In fact, most written job descriptions are full of nothing *but* minimal expectations.

You will show up on time, you will do these tasks, you will meet these minimal measures, and you will answer to these people. What's more, most job descriptions are based on minimal expectations—they are not written with high performing employees or over-achievers in mind, at all.

In fact, the way that most job descriptions are worded makes them sound as though they were written with the presumption that without these written minimal standards, an employee would not even try to work up to the mark.

They are written as though they assume that any employee would try to do the *least* amount of work possible on any given day if these lists of responsibilities were not provided for them.

Not exactly the basis for an inspiring, mutually beneficial relationship, is it?

There is nothing particularly fulfilling about meeting minimal standards as an employee.

And the other side of the equation is just as bad, because there is nothing about an employer-employee agreement for meeting minimal standards (in exchange for pay) that lends itself to continuous improvement and the pursuit of excellence, the pursuit of extra-ordinary.

Here is what I propose instead, from both sides of the employee/employer relationship: don't work jobs.

Instead, no matter what your job, set out to work your calling.

So what's the difference?

A job is something you can do (a competence) and probably something you have to do for financial reasons; but your calling is something you *want* to do (a passion). And the two are not necessarily mutually exclusive.

Many times people think of callings as grand vocations—the reason that people become doctors or ministers or public servants. But those are not callings, those are jobs, roles that people are drawn to because they are called to help and heal, called to spread a message that is bigger than themselves, called to give assistance to people who cannot help themselves, etc. In other words, their calling is facilitated by the role they chose to use to fulfill it.

No matter what your job is, you can still work your calling.

Think of your calling as those things you most love doing, those things that give you the most personal satisfaction, those things that stimulate your creativity and passion. And no matter what your job, work your calling.

This might require that you revisit the terms of your employment and negotiate with your boss to modify your job in ways that will allow this. It might even require that you seek a new role within your organization or outside of it.

If you have proven yourself not only against the minimal standards of your job description but as someone who is willing to exceed them, your employer may be open to discussing how your role could be modified relative to your passions—the things you feel called to do.

If you are an employer, you should grab onto this concept as well.

If you write employment terms in traditional job descriptions and manage and measure your employees by a set of minimal standards, that is exactly what you can expect to have: employees who return the minimum. That is all you have the right to require; it's all you have promised to pay for.

If you really want to get more from your employees, provide the means by which that can happen!

You have to be willing to take a chance on people. Demonstrate that you trust your staff to not only do what is expected, but that you trust them to work from their passions to do more.

Help employees discover their passions and strengths and then work creatively to craft roles by which they can exercise them. And reward and acknowledge people in return for the investment that they make with their passions—the contributions that come from their hearts and souls.

Can you imagine working for a company like this?

Can you imagine providing a workplace like this?

Can you imagine running your company like this, and all of the places that employees who worked their calling instead of just their competence could take your business?

"Do not stop thinking of life as an adventure.
You have no security unless ...you can choose a challenge instead of a competence."

(Eleanor Roosevelt (1884–1962) First Lady, American humanitarian and UN diplomat)

Little White Marketing Lie #3:

"Word of mouth is our best marketing."

Unfortunately, for most of the business owners making this claim it's true—but by default.

Because what they are really saying is that they have idea what else—if anything—in their marketing mix is producing any results, at all.

Or worse, word-of-mouth marketing is actually the *only* form of marketing in which they are engaged.

And even *that* is a little white marketing lie because:

> (1) 'you' cannot do word of mouth marketing. By definition, your customers do it for you and you have no control over whether or how it occurs. And,

> (2) your clients are not going to walk out of your business and spontaneously talk about your business to others unless and until you give them something to talk about!

In reality, most business owners who make this claim are engaging not in word of mouth marketing, but in what I call **"accidental marketing."**

When pressed to reveal your definition of word of mouth marketing, you reveal that what "word of mouth marketing" means to you is that you feel that the products, services or experience you provide your customers is *so* amazing that they simply cannot wait to go and tell everyone they know about how wonderful you are.

(Oh yes, and how you provide exceptional customer service because of how your employees set you apart.)

That is not word of mouth marketing, that is accidental marketing.

In fact, it's not even accidental marketing—that would imply some kind of action on your part.

For most business owners who claim that word of mouth is their best marketing, it really means that they are *doing almost nothing* when it comes to marketing but still somehow hoping for *accidental* success.

To give you an idea of how effective it is, would you do accidental bookkeeping, hoping that customers would remember to pay you, and pay you the right amount, without giving them a bill? Accidental accounting? Tax reporting?

Accidental purchasing to stock your wares? Accidental programming?

Would you provide services to your clients by accident—without consultation to find out what they need, without education, and without strategy?

There are many facets of your business you approach strategically and intentionally, many of which you perform on a daily or even an hourly basis, and for which you have written detailed procedures and policies.

There are aspects of business in which you have invested countless hours and thousands of dollars in education and training.

In some areas you believe to be important and for which you know there are not shortcuts, you dedicate the time and energy required to do them properly or even outsource them to more qualified professionals.

But somehow, when it comes to *marketing*, your actions reveal that you don't truly believe marketing is a legitimate, important part of your business planning and operations.

Marketing should receive the same level of focus and attention that all of the other components of your business do—from your professional education to your bookkeeping and billing to your products and services—but for many small businesses, it does not.

Are you employing the type of strategy where you open your doors and wait for the phone to ring, wondering where all the customers are?

Where you invest thousands of dollars in genuinely superior retail products which end up sitting on the shelves collecting dust waiting for a chance to "sell themselves?"

Where as an independent professional or small business owner, you wonder why your landlord is not out there getting business to walk in the door for you?

If so, you are, in fact, not marketing, but hoping for accidental success.

Meanwhile, businesses which are actively engaged in the strategic, targeted marketing needed to build a successful business know that it takes actual, intentional action in order to produce a result (*and they are going to leave 'accidental marketers' in the dust!*)

In fact, accidental marketing—doing nothing but hoping that your customers are out there making referrals anyway—is not even a legitimate word of mouth marketing strategy.

Because to generate word of mouth referrals, invitations, and buzz, you have to do something that is, in fact, buzz-worthy.

Waiting for business to come to you by chance might feel safer and more comfortable to you, and you might even be able to lie to yourself, since a few customers send referrals your way once in a while by telling yourself it's proof that you have "word of mouth" marketing going on.

But this is just about the least effective strategy you can employ to build your business.

For the sake of clarity (and so you will know whether or not you are actually engaged in or stimulating any actual legitimate word-of-mouth marketing tactics) here are definitions for the terms we commonly refer to as word of mouth marketing:

- **Word of Mouth Marketing:** simply the passing of information about your business from person to person. Often confused with doing nothing yet hoping people will accidentally talk about you or your business—remember, people will not talk about your business unless and until you give them something to talk about!

- **Buzz Marketing:** a word-of-mouth marketing technique wherein a business tries to make interactions with customers appear to be unique, spontaneous exchanges of information, rather than delivery of pre-scripted marketing pitches.

- **Viral marketing:** "...is an idea that spreads... and while spreading actually helps market your business or cause." (Seth Godin, sethgodin.typepad.com)

- **Grassroots marketing:** when volunteers are organized and motivated to engage in personal outreach

- **Community marketing:** creating or identifying existing communities made up of people with shared interests, values, etc., and conducting marketing efforts within those niche, targeted communities

- **Evangelist or brand advocate marketing:** identifying and developing individuals who are passionate about your business and encouraging and empowering them to spread the word on behalf of your business or cause

- **Seeding the market:** Putting product or product samples into the hands of individuals who are influencers and likely to spread the word about your business

- **Cause marketing:** supporting local or national causes or holding charitable events which are of interest to your most important clients or ideal client types in order to create a shared value and to benefit the cause, while also creating positive buzz or even business for your own organization

- **Referral programs:** inducements for people to refer other people to your business

- **Influencer marketing:** identifying and wooing (and sometimes even paying or otherwise rewarding) key individuals, opinion leaders, social media influencers, and other similar types who would be likely to talk about your business and who are likely to influence a significant number of your target market to visit your business or make a purchase

Still think word of mouth marketing is your best marketing?

Actually, it should be.

It *should be* true that your customers are treated to extraordinary experiences by employees they would not find anywhere else. It should be true. And if it were, you would have the kind of real word of mouth referral marketing that you have dreamed of.

But if you have determined that it's not, it's time to step back and take a look at every customer touch point to see where the client experience can be improved and made special. It's time to step back and see whether your employees believe in the mission and vision of your organization, whether they share your authentic core values, and whether their jobs are tied to the fulfillment of the former, by means of the latter.

And it's time to step back and create a real, formal marketing plan. One that ensures the brand of your business is being consistently represented across all channels and touch points, and one that is strategic.

Like every other vital component to your business operations, there just isn't a shortcut.

Following are elements common to formal marketing plans. Whether you hire a consultant to take you through the process or conduct your own exercise, make their review part of your annual planning process. Common components of formal business marketing plans:

- **Situational Analysis**
  1. External environment
  2. Your corporate mission, vision, shared values, long and short range goals and objectives
  3. Current status: position, products, services, client types, market share, distribution, pricing, packaging, marketing
  4. Competitive analysis
  5. Customer / consumer analysis
  6. Brand review

- **SWOT Analysis** (Strengths, Weaknesses, Opportunities, Threats)

- **Strategic Marketing Plan**
  1. Identify objectives and goals
  2. List current strategies
  3. Describe ideal client types and identify target markets
  4. Refine Competitive Advantages and Unique Selling Proposition/s
  5. Positioning
  6. Branding

- **Marketing Mix**
  1. Creation of Strategy and Tactics
  2. Product
  3. Distribution
  4. Pricing
  5. Promotion
  6. Communications
  7. Assumptions
  8. Budget, Timing, Assignment of Responsibilities
  9. Plan and Timing for Periodic Assessment/s

- **Implementation of the Plan**

- **Measurement, Evaluation and Adjustments**

Little White Marketing Lie #4:

"Our customers love us."

Don't fall for this little white marketing lie; it's especially dangerous.

When you begin to believe that your customers need, want or even love your business more than your business needs, wants and shows that they love your customers, you are in trouble.

You are just a hop, skip and a jump from complacency, neglect or even a level of condescending disdain that will reveal just how fragile that customer relationship was.

By nearly every measure, you cannot support the claim that your customers love you.

To understand why, you have to know what characterizes true love:

Love is unselfish and patient.

It is slow to take offense and overlooks shortcomings.

Love puts the interests of the object of its love ahead of its own interests.

Those who love are almost unconditionally faithful to the object of their affection.

If this describes your customers, I want to know where you live and I want to know how I can get me some!

The truth is, customers are self-centered. They are in the relationship for what they are getting out of it. *And why shouldn't they be?*

They are likely to take offense and notice shortcomings.

If their interests change, they will go elsewhere.

And they are fickle. Most are more than open to the possibility of being wooed by another offer and many welcome any opportunity to experience something new.

The truth is, you customers are all dressed up for a night out on the town. They are sitting at the proverbial bar, made up, and looking especially desirable. And they are just waiting for someone else to buy them a drink.

There is a way to get customer love, but it's going to cost you.

Why? Your customers are never going to put more into the relationship than you do.

I call this the Law of Reflection:

> Imagine a still pool of water providing a reflection.
> The reflection on the water may be a fair image of the
> original, but the original is still by far the strongest,
> clearest side.

Like it or not, the "love" bestowed on your business by any of your customers is only a direct reflection of your dedication to, engagement with, and interest in, them.

You will never get more than you invest and your customers will never love you more than you truly love them (at least not for long).

The love you show for the customer is the original, their response is the reflection. Just like a reflection in a clear pool of water, the reflection is never going to be stronger than the original!

Just as in other relationships, there are some ways to gain and nurture mutual affection:

- Remember the fickle nature of customers' love and stay on top of your game.

- Deliver great customer experiences, every time.

- Be intriguing, engaging and provocative.

- Keep your eyes and ears open for signs of discontent.

- Communicate, proactively. Solicit feedback.

- Listen. No, I mean really listen.

- Respond to customer's complaints, wants and needs.

- Be open to change. Ask how you can change. When your customer tells you that you need to change, by all means, change!

- Get help from professionals when you need it.

And maybe most importantly: establish emotional connections—give people reasons to love you.

- Tell the story of your business.

- Create passionate brand advocates through extraordinary customer experiences—this means you have done something that is really meaningful to them or that even changes their lives for the better—as a result of doing business with you. Share testimonials.

- Passion is contagious! Tell people why you are passionate about 'what you do,' why you feel called to the business or industry in which you are engaged or what really excites you about your field of expertise.

- Talk about your family history and other connections to the community.

- Tell customers about the good that your business does in the lives of community members and employees.

- Educate the public about the ways in which your business benefits the local economy, local charities, schools, the arts and other organizations.

- Give your customers emotional reasons to care about whether or not your business does well through your affiliation and support of local causes, local schools, or other community or philanthropic efforts.

It's never about you or your business; it's always about your customers, when it comes to your relationship with them.

Don't fall for the lie that your customers love you, or that they need you even nearly as much as you need them. Instead, stay focused on providing benefits and value to your customers, and focus your marketing on telling customers about how doing business with you makes their lives better.

More?

Here is the secret to cultivating customer loyalty—with every customer that walks in your door.

What makes customers and employees develop loyalty to you is (drum roll please....) your loyalty to them.

You earn loyalty by meeting and exceeding customers' needs in such a way that they perceive to be irreplaceable, over and over again, over time. There is no shortcut to loyalty and there are no guarantees that, once gained, loyalty will endure; loyalty can be eroded more quickly than it can be built.

If it's so much work, is it worth it?

Absolutely.

Loyal customers will buy your stuff, and will buy more of your stuff and loyal customers will keep coming back again and again to buy even more of your stuff.

Loyal customers will not buy your competitor's stuff.

Loyal customers will refer their friends, family, co-workers and acquaintances to you.

Loyal customers will even talk to perfect strangers about you—they'll sing your praises to anyone they think you can help.

Loyal customers will provide you with great testimonials and helpful feedback.

Loyal customers will identify themselves with your brand on social media networks.

Don't fall for the misconception that you can garner customer loyalty through price.

While discounting has been the name of the game for the last couple of years once the effects of the recession really started to hurt the US consumer, discounting does **not** breed loyalty.

Once your lower your price, a competitor is sure to follow, and you find yourself undermining the vitality of your own organization with absolutely nothing to show for it.

As those who jumped in to location-based internet offers have quickly learned, most bargain shoppers are loyal to just one thing: **the discount.**

Many small business owners who tried deep discounts to get customers through the door or lowered prices and then marketed the heck out of their price point advantage are left scratching their heads because **what they believed to be true, was not true.**

They believed that their products or services were totally relevant, that their facility was acceptable, that their staff were qualified and competent.

They believed that if they could get them in the door once, they would come back again. **But it did not happen.**

So why *didn't* they convert the leads provided to them by way of location based deals?

One (or more) of their assumptions was not correct.

And ultimately, the final answer is that (for whatever reason) the customer experience created was simply not compelling enough to stimulate customer intrigue.

Intrigue, you ask?

I thought we were talking about loyalty?

We are!

Creating intrigue is the first step to any long-term, loyal relationship with a customer.

Here is why:

> **Intrigue** (*verb; meaning*)
> to fascinate, arouse the curiosity of, or amuse.
> (http://www.thefreedictionary.com/intrigue)

It might help to think of it this way; you invest thousands and thousands of dollars on your facility, personnel, products and training, and you invest even more than that in time and energy.

But the customer only sees a microscopic portion of that investment.

Some part of the minutes or hours that they spend in direct interaction with your business (whether that experience occurs online or between "real people" in a physical business location) must trigger intrigue in them in order for customer to want to come back and in order for them to want to try something else that you have to offer.

The editors of television reality shows condense what they feel are the most compelling, provocative, exciting and important conversations, activities and events that occur over the course of a week or even longer, into a one or two hour-long show. That might mean distilling upwards of 168 hours (more than ten thousand minutes) into just 35 or 40 minutes of actual show time, minus commercials and "coming up next" teasers.

They try to produce the most *intriguing,* engaging and provocative episode possible in order to entice viewers to watch the show again, to follow contestants, to visit their web sites and, in some cases, even to decide the outcome of the series via public vote.

In the same way, you have to think about and view each client visit as though it were their own personal condensed, exaggerated reality show—because it is.

In other words, your client will see, hear, smell and otherwise experience the elements that you—intentionally or unintentionally—edit down into the block of time they are present within your business.

Now that you know you are the producer and real time editor of the customer experience, how can you orchestrate each one to be intriguing to every customer who walks through your door?

How can you make them want to become regular viewers?

How can you stimulate their curiosity to try other products or services?

How can you interest them enough to tell their friends and family to tune in to your show?

CHAPTER BONUS:

More on the law of reflection

How many times have you wondered what it would take to turn one time customers into repeat customers, to turn repeat customers into exclusively loyal ones—to attract and develop a small army of influential people who are eager to refer, recommend and otherwise talk about your brand to others?

How many times have you felt powerless and hopeless when it comes to getting your employees to think more like stakeholders—people who have a vested interest in the health and well-being of the company? So that they are engaged and loyal to the business, not just the paycheck, and make decisions that are in the best interest of the company, even if it's not always comfortable or most convenient for themselves?

How many times have you wondered why you are not converting more search engine results, blog post links and other web site visitors into online sales and in-store visits?

Here is the secret.

People don't buy from companies, they buy from people.

People don't develop loyalty to companies, they become loyal—and sometimes even addicted—to ways companies make their lives better or how they make them feel as a result of doing business with them.

Getting found by search engines, having your blog posts read and getting people to your website is a preliminary step; only what happens after that point—the engagement and emotional connection built into the online experience—produces sales, booked appointments and in-store visits.

Only what occurs **after** someone walks into your store in terms of engagement and emotional connection produces desired results at the cash register, repeat visits and referrals.

Employees will not think like stakeholders when they are treated like "tools."

And all of it can be attributed to what I call the Law of Reflection.

Here is its shortest, sweetest version:

> No one invest more into your relationships than you.

Employees will not invest themselves personally in the well-being of your company until they feel that you are invested in them.

Clocking in does not produce engagement, and a paycheck doesn't entitle you to love and devotion (let alone referrals or over-the-top performance).

If you want employees to act like stakeholders, you have to give them reasons to feel like one, first.

Customers will not become loyal to you until you become loyal to them, making them #1 in your focus and thinking, and making it your goal to benefit them and improve their lives.

(Notice how "sell stuff to them" is nowhere to be found in that statement.)

The relationship and loyalties that customers develop toward you and your business is a direct reflection of your commitment to and interest in them.

Likewise, the loyalty and engagement employees demonstrate toward your business is a direct reflection of not only your policies and employee culture but also of how much (or little) you really invest in them in terms of education and training, and of how important you make them feel that they are to you, and to the success, future and welfare of your business.

Understanding the Law of Reflection is the first step on the road to loyalty and engagement, changing the way that you think about your business and set goals and priorities must follow.

Remember, just like with a pool of water, the reflection (how customers or employees feel about you and your business) is never going to be clearer or stronger than the original, and you are the one responsible for creating the original side of those relationships.

Little White Marketing Lie #5:

"Success is just one great idea away."

Most of the time, 'instant success' is achieved only after years and years of hard work and much trial and error. It's not about one great idea.

Success is usually the result of trying one more time, and one more time after that.

It's about experimenting, refining and continually improving.

It's about demanding the best of yourself, and then asking for a little bit more.

And history is on my side on this one.

As Thomas Edison, the famous U.S. inventor who was awarded more than 1,000 patents in his lifetime and among whose inventions are the electric light bulb, the storage battery, the electric generator, the steam locomotive engine, the microphone and many other that have radically changed our culture and lives for the better once famously said,

> "Genius is 2% inspiration and 98% perspiration."

And maybe he said it even better in his autobiography when he simply stated,

> "There is no substitute for hard work."

And that is precisely why so many people *prefer* to believe the myth that it will be a great idea that brings them success—after all—who wants to work hard? And who wants to fail, repeatedly in the process?

Because that is exactly what Thomas Edison did, and if you want to succeed, you will adopt his mentality.

He did not view himself as a failure, even though he failed hundreds of times while trying to invent the light bulb. When questioned as to the hundreds of failures he had while trying to invent the light bulb he said he hadn't failed, he had merely succeeded in determining what *did not* work.

Knowing what *doesn't* work is important, too.

Knowing what doesn't work keeps you from going down the wrong roads, chasing phantoms (apparitions like the myth of "instant success.")

The truth is, you are probably closer to success than you realize. You *already had* a great idea, that is why you are in business. And even if the idea of your business is not unique in and of itself, how you do business can be.

There are not shortcuts and there are few serendipitous 'post-it-note' accidental discoveries that result in overnight business super-stardom. Not to mention the fact that you don't want to go down in history as a one-hit wonder!

History is replete with companies that had a great idea or business concept and started strong, but got stuck.

Take Steve Jobs, for example, who said, "Stay hungry, stay foolish," speaking at a commencement address Year after year, project after project, Steve Job's company and products took the market by surprise, and by storm. Without believing in the vision of something that did not even exist yet, and then demanding and fostering the uniquely innovative internal culture required to produce them, it is likely that his great ideas would have become someone else's on which to capitalize.

For most successful businesses, the secret is not in having a great idea; it's:

- Doing things right, over and over again, and doing them differently than the others.

- Making it easier for customers to shop or buy.

- Providing a better, more convenient way for customers to purchase what they want.

- Providing customers with a better value for the things they want.

It's not what they do, it's how they do it.

Lands End? Zappos? Again, there is nothing particularly innovative about selling shoes or clothes. But these businesses are genius—and consequently successful—because of the way they fulfill orders, the way they stand behind their products and the culture they provide for their employees. Believing that happy employees will translate into happy customers, they built their policies and business around this core value.

So don't focus on trying to come up with a genius new idea or offering.

Instead, channel the bulk of your creative energies into **perfecting the customer experience** your business provides by:

(1) delivering on your promises to the customer, every time; and,

(2) making the customer experience at your business unique, different from competitors and more than the customer expects, in ways that are attractive and meaningful to your customers.

Persistence may be more important to your success almost anything else. But don't just take my word for it, smarter people than me agree. Next time you are tempted to quit, or quit an initiative without seeing it all the way through, remind yourself:

"Never, never, never give up."
(Winston Churchill)

"Ambition is the path to success.
Persistence is the vehicle you arrive in."
(Bill Bradley)

"Energy and persistence conquer all things."
(Benjamin Franklin)

"The habit of persistence is the habit of victory."
(Herbert Kaufman)

"Paralyze resistance with persistence."
(Woody Hayes)

"Success is almost totally dependent upon **drive and persistence**. The extra energy required to **make another effort** or try another approach is the secret of winning."
(Dennis Waitley)

"And **let us not grow weary** of doing good,
for in due season we will reap, if we **do not give up**."
(Paul the Apostle, Galatians 6:9)

Sometimes the only difference between the successful and those who are not is persistence.

Showing up, trying, doing, learning, putting what was learned into practice, and showing up again, the next day.

If you want to be successful, persist.

Through your demonstrated commitment to your business, its values and the mission and vision statements you claim to believe in, make persistence one of the defining traits of your character, a word that those closest to you would use to describe you.

Do not give up in pursuit of your dream or in doing what you know is right, because you will never have or enjoy the first without the second.

Little White Marketing Lie #6:

"Marketing is a verb."

Have you ever wondered how important marketing really is to the life of your business? That is like asking how important breathing is to your body!

No matter what you want to do or what it is your business provides, marketing is the means to that end. And it's not just important—marketing impacts, and is impacted by, everything about your business.

You might even say that everything about your business is marketing. **Why?**

Because each and every time a client comes into contact with you or any aspect of your business, each and every interaction works together to paint a picture in the customer or prospect's mind about you and your business.

Is the picture being painted in all of these encounters all you hope or intend for it to be?

Stop thinking that "marketing" is a verb or an activity or a set of activities—things that you should be (or should start) doing.

Marketing is not a verb. A verb implies action that begins and ends. And many people think that the purpose of marketing is to stimulate sales. Wrong again!

Everything about your business *is* marketing:

Many business owners fail to realize is that everything is marketing. (That's marketing with a small "m," not a large one.)

I am not saying that marketing should be the most important among your responsibilities or departments (if you are lucky enough to have "people" to do marketing activities for you!), but I am suggesting that you need to change the way that you think about and define "marketing" in your business.

Everything that directly or indirectly impacts the customer experience in any way—retailing, communications, policies, staff and the employee culture, training, advertising, events, your management style, décor, pricing, merchandising— everything must be viewed as part of your marketing.

Marketing is not about stimulating sales, it's about motivating people.

And yes, marketing is about motivating people to visit your business, to find out more about your products or services and to make purchases.

But it's also about motivating your employees to provide the best possible experience for your customers. It's about your priorities when it comes to hiring the individuals who will be responsible to fulfill that customer experience. It's about the culture—the feeling and personality of your business—you want to create.

Advertisements? Websites? Events? Mailers? Social media and other tools? They are just that: Tools.

In and of themselves, marketing tools don't constitute marketing, because they cannot work to the best of their ability (or even at all) if you don't understand and believe that everything about your business is marketing.

Set aside the preconceived ideas and perceptions that you have when you think of the word "marketing." It's not a department. It's not promotional or advertising activities. It's not a website, event, mailer, Facebook page or Yellow Pages ad.

Want to know what marketing really *is*?

"Marketing" is anything and everything you do to **attract, engage, retain or motivate customers**. It encompasses everything that in any way impacts the customer experience, at any touch point, for better or for worse.

Therefore, by extension, everyone within your company is 'in' marketing.

Not convinced? Here is what I mean:

- The dust left on products, the half-cleaned spill, the dirty bathroom or overflowing trash cans left by your cleaning staff says more to clients about how much you care about them and how proud you are of your business than any words you can say.

- The clutter of disorganized shopping areas and cardboard boxes left unpacked in the aisles represents obstacles to your customers that may prevent sales. Clutter and disorganization also makes some people feel so uncomfortable that they might not return at all.

- The "breaking news" on your website that is months (or even years) old tells customers and prospective customers you are not savvy or concerned enough to keep it updated.

- No one in your company actually knows your corporate mission or vision, so each interprets it in their own way (if they think about it at all).

- Your employee culture is characterized by cynicism rather than enthusiasm when it comes to corporate goals and objectives. People roll their eyes when you talk about change. In fact, one or more of your staff members resists change at all costs, rather than embracing change and pursuing continuous improvement.

- Employees are actually scolded (or worse) for going above and beyond on behalf of a customer in violation of even minor policies; with the result that no one is willing to think creatively to solve customer problems.

But those are fairly obvious, are not they? How about these:

- The sign taped to your cash register by your accountant announcing a new financial policy that effectively tells all of your customers that everyone is going to be 'punished' because one person failed to be honest. (For that matter, when was the last time you looked at the invoices being sent out to customers—do they include more negatively toned rules and disclaimers than the paperwork you signed to get your last business loan?)

- The sign posted on your door telling customers their kids are not welcome inside.

- The new check out protocol that gives your purchasing department more information but represents confusion, delay and frustration for staff and customers at the cash register and makes your customers leery of just how much information you really have on them.

- The memo sent by human resources to your employees noting that since the cost of insurance is going up, their benefits are going down, resulting in a loss of morale.

- The loyalty and rewards program that never really rewards the customer.

- The manager (or any other employee) who puts obstacles in the way of others, who resists and pooh-poohs corporate initiatives and territorially hoards information as a way to maintain perceived power.

And it's not always the things that you do, sometimes it's what you fail to do:

- Some of the contact information on your business card changed, but instead of ordering new business cards, you crossed it out and wrote on it by hand so that you would not waste a few dollars worth of business cards.

  In doing this (or presenting customers with any other collateral with outdated, obsolete information, menu items that are no longer offered, etc.,) you not only demonstrate a lack of concern over your presentation to customers, you might even be telling them that you are so unsuccessful that you cannot afford to update your collateral, or that you are so temporary that they might as well wait and see whether you will still be around next month. Not exactly the way to inspire customer confidence, is it?

- You asked customers to subscribe to emails but never sent one.

- You started a blog but never posted.

- You launched a Facebook page but never change your status or answer customer inquiries.

- Your suggestion box (whether for customers or employees) has never been opened, or if it was, the requests were so outdated that they were tossed.

- No one bothers to acknowledge, thank or contact people who made suggestions.

- The lack of orientation and training for new employees resulting in poor customer experiences while staff learn "on the job," using customers as guinea pigs.

- Employees who don't know (and cannot be bothered to learn) how to properly direct customers outside of their own job or department.

- You never ask for, incentivize or in any way solicit referrals.

- Your failure to genuinely and frequently acknowledge, recognize and thank your employees; or worse,

- You left the culture and climate of your business up to chance (or up to others), with the result that your employee culture is rife with gossip, jealousy, insecurity and in-fighting—sometimes even in front of your customers.

I am not suggesting that the Marketing Director should be the real CEO of your company, or that you need a degree in Marketing in order to succeed in business.

I am saying that **everyone** in your organization, from the CEO and ownership on down, must cultivate a customer-centric mindset—a "marketing mindset," if you will.

There is no part of your business and no staff member within your business whose activities and functionality does not impact the customer experience, whether directly or indirectly.

From your operating policies to employee morale to the appearance of your brick-and-mortar or online business sites, everything affects the customer perception about your business, for better or for worse.

If you are ready to build an organization where each member of your team seeks to provide the best possible experience for customers at each and every touch point, you get it!

- Revisit the mission and vision of your company.

- Working with staff, create a customer bill of rights and ask staff members to commit to upholding it.

- Make sure that each member of your team understands how the role that they play impacts the customer experience and how it specifically works toward fulfillment of your corporate mission and vision statement.

- Tie incentives, salaries and performance evaluations to the customer experience.

- Solicit customer feedback (and make use of it!)

- Embrace change and continuous improvement.

Everything about your business is marketing. Whether you act on that knowledge strategically or leave it all up to chance, is up to you!

CHAPTER BONUS:

Make sure marketing is more than a "Girl Friday"

I love old movies and watched a ton of them as a kid, so the term "gal Friday" is one I have heard before. Do you know what a 'Gal Friday' is? I not only know from the movies, I know what it is from personal experience, because I have been one, more than once.

A "Girl Friday" is that person in the office frequently tapped to un-jam the copier, replace the toner or run the postage machine. They order office supplies, bounce out to pick up food for the important people, clean up after the meetings they probably took the notes for, and make all the emergency runs to the office supplies store for paper, ink or other items.

A "Girl Friday" is someone often treated as though they exist professionally for the convenience and benefit of others, with little thought to what their official job and real responsibilities really are (or should be). They often bear a title including the word "assistant."

And assist they do!

Because they are amiable and willing (or at least obliged and expected) to help out with whatever needs to be done, they are often taken for granted, undervalued, and their real skills and strengths get overlooked.

In too many businesses, Marketing is treated like a 'Gal Friday.'

And as a result, Marketing is taken for granted, under or mis-utilized and its most powerful, effective strengths and abilities are wasted.

Too often, Marketing:

- is viewed as the 'errand girl' for the Sales Department or the public relations conduit for the CEO or head of Finance.

- is appealed to for help to 'un-jam' the company from mistakes made.

- is brought in to try to 'clean out' items that Purchasing shouldn't have purchased or shouldn't have purchased so many of.

- is called upon at the last minute to make an emergency attempt to help fill up classes and events or promote products that did not magically sell themselves, as had been predicted would occur.

If, as I suggest, Marketing includes all the activities, means and tools you use to:

1. **attract** customers,

2. **engage** customers,

3. **motivate** customers (to take specific actions you want them to take, such as making referrals or more expensive purchases), and

4. **retain** customers,

then Marketing deserves a seat at the table in your business, from the get-go. Marketing deserves the attention needed to form a strategic, measurable plan. Marketing deserves the allocation of a budget, resources and measurements.

Marketing is not your "Girl Friday," there only to facilitate or clean up after others.

If you treat Marketing like an afterthought in your business—like a "tool" you use only to try to achieve the ends of others—then you are wasting its strengths and you don't really understand Marketing, at all.

And if that is true, can you really expect Marketing to work for you, at all?

Little White Marketing Lie #7:

"We need to tell people how great we are."

If you have been in business very long, it's likely you have had to create scripts and write marketing copy for your website, advertisements, signs, postcards or other items which fall under the general heading, "marketing collateral."

And no doubt you have taken the opportunity to talk about the things you love most about your business, or the things you think other people would most appreciate about your business, your products, your employees, etc.

But the truth is, for the most part, your marketing collateral and scripts shouldn't talk about your business at all.

Apart from your actual call to action or telling people where to obtain the solutions you provide, your marketing content should 'talk about' your customers and prospects.

Ironically, you probably went into business in the first place for people-oriented reasons; you wanted to provide solutions people need and want. And while you have not lost sight of your calling, this is not what is being reflected in your marketing; and as a result, your marketing is not connecting with those you most desire that it should.

To look at most advertising and marketing copy, you would think that businesses believe that they are their own reason for existing. Most marketing copy seems to imply that customers should count themselves lucky to be able to get their products or services—that they should feel lucky to be able to call themselves customers at all.

Somewhere along the line, people lost track of what is really at the heart of the matter: the wants and needs of their customers.

Effective marketing speaks to customer needs and wants.

When you talk about your business, you are more likely to be thinking from the standpoint of what your business needs and wants (customers and sales) vs. what your customers and prospects truly need and want.

It goes back to a question I have posed before:

Do you really want to make your customers happy by identifying and gratifying *their* tastes, appetites and desires; or, do you want to essentially compel your customers to be happy with what *you* want them to be happy with?

Take time to make a list of the things that your customers most need and want (this may require that you do some market research) that your business provides:

- problems they have (that your business solves)

- what they desire (that your business provides)

- what they value in their customer experiences

And then write marketing copy that connects with them, by demonstrating a clear understanding of *their* needs and wants—copy that puts you all "in the same boat," so to speak.

Once you have their attention and you have shown them that you understand what they really want and need, point out how your business can meet those wants and needs.

Design your marketing to talk not about your business or your own personal amazing-ness; instead, focus on the benefits the customer can expect as a result of using your products or services, and as a result of doing business with you.

How does doing business with you make your customer's lives better?

Great marketing keeps the spotlight on the true star of your business story: the customer!

Get engaged

To succeed in business during the coming years, you are going to have to engage with your customers like never before, using more means of communication than ever before.

And just like any other engagement, you will never get engaged if you don't ever meet—so you will need to 'be' where your customers 'are.'

Once you have found them, you need to engage them. To engage them, you need to understand what it means:

>**en-gage**: (*verb, meaning*)
>
>1. To involve oneself or become occupied; participate: engage in conversation.
>
>2. To assume an obligation; agree.
>
>3. To enter into conflict or battle, as in, "The armies engaged at dawn."
>
>4. To become meshed or interlocked, as in, "The gears engaged."

Look at the definition; it's almost a picture of the customer life cycle.

- One, become involved (the prospect finds you, or you find them, and an interaction occurs).

- Two, assume an obligation (they agree to pay, you agree to provide services and/or products in return).

- Three, to enter into conflict or battle (sure, it's a stretch, but I am going to liken this to the customer, becoming involved in your battle—to grow your business—by telling others about you or choosing to purchase from you again).

- And four, to become meshed or interlocked: based on 1-3, you now have developed customer loyalty and even brand advocacy.

To do *any* of that, you need to know them (both your current and desired/ideal customers).

You need to have an idea of the shared interests, values and passions of your current customers, and you need to have an idea of those of your ideal client types (those you most want to attract, or want to be able to attract in the future) as well.

Engagement—and the potential to move someone through to the next level of engagement—occurs any time you come into contact with a prospect or customer. That means that opportunities for engagement will occur both within your business and without.

The interactions that will engage people—get them to want to do business with you, to want to do business with you again, to want to tell others about you, and to want to do business only with you (when it comes to the products and services you provide)—these types of interactions will be those where alignment of emotional connection and relevance (what you have is actually something your customers need) occurs.

Make now the moment you set out to truly connect with your customers.

Find out where they live, what they truly want and need, what stirs their passions, what things they believe in, what they value in and about your community, and so on.

So go ahead, get engaged—it's going to be a great year!

Little White Marketing Lie #8:

"It takes luck to get a great team."

At some point your have probably seen one of those sports movies where some under-achieving coach who is past their prime finds themselves stuck with a bunch of players other teams had rejected or who had retired years before. And somehow that rag-tag bunch of clowns starts winning and—against all odds and logic—becomes a champion no one thought they could be.

News flash:
That is not how it works in real life.

If you want to have a great team, you are going to have to do what it takes to build it and you are going to have to take the actions that great teams take and lead like great leaders lead.

So what is it that sets great teams apart?

What is it that great teams do differently and better than the others?

I identified fourteen things that great teams do better than the others while analyzing teams during the last NFL playoff season.

Cultivating these traits within your business and employee culture will give you a competitive advantage and put you in a position to gain ground when it comes to sales, customer loyalty and employee engagement.

What's more, it will make your business stronger—more successful not only in the short term but better prepared for the long haul.

So here are my 14 characteristics of great teams for business success:

1. Great teams study the competition. They scout opposing players and analyze the play of other teams. They discover the strengths of the other team and they look for weaknesses they can exploit for competitive advantage.

- Do you know who your competitors are? Do you know what they are best at? Do you know what their 'fans' love most about them? Do you know what their weaknesses are?

- The answers to these questions can help you develop tactics to improve your own performance to better compete. And by analyzing their weaknesses, you can gain not only competitive advantage but you may also be able to identify portions of your shared target markets which they are not serving well.

In other words, rather than competing against the competition at their points of strength, take advantage in areas where they are weak or may have completely overlooked.

2. Great teams strategize and plan. They spend hours and hours and hours "off the field" creating detailed game plans and even contingency plans for the team to follow on the field.

- Do you have a plan? Do you have a mission and vision statement? Do you have a customer bill of rights?

  Do all of your employees know the plan, understand your mission and vision, support the promises you make to customers and—most importantly—understand how their role helps to fulfill each?

  When was the last time you conducted a SWOT analysis? (SWOT=Strengths, Opportunities, Weaknesses, Threats)

- Do you even have a marketing plan, or are you winging it? Do you have specific goals for sales, new customer acquisition, retention, referrals, customer life cycle management and strategies to achieve them? Have you identified measures and are you gauging progress against your goals on a regular basis?

- Do you have contingency plans for when things go awry, competitors emerge, the market changes or emergencies occur?

3. Great teams work as a team. While players who carry, catch or throw the ball might get more time in the spotlight, they represent only a small fraction of the players on the team, most of whom rarely touch the ball at all. On great teams, those in the spotlight understand that they can only do what they do because of the efforts of their teammates who perform other roles.

On great teams, **every team member** understands their own role and how it contributes to the success of the team as a whole. They know the importance of what they do and they strive, continually, to improve. And every team member has an appreciation for the contributions of their team-mates; they know that everyone is needed for team success.

- Few businesses of any size can say that all or most of their team members perform at this level; it's likely that there are few businesses where even a significant portion of their employees perform at this level.

To develop this type of employee culture:

- Make sure all employees know the game plan: the mission and vision of your company, the promises you make to customers, the values which guide your policies, your business goals and long term objectives.

- Make sure that all employees study the play book: the strategies and tactics that will be employed in order to fulfill the mission and vision of the organization fulfill customer promises and reach goals.

- Every employee must understand how their job works to fulfill the mission and vision of the organization, how it enhances and impacts the customer experience and how what they do impacts the ability of others in the organization to succeed.

- Create a culture where each employee feels equally valuable and needed by the organization. Don't misunderstand, I am not talking about money. What I mean is that in many organizations, one or more departments or individuals feels (or allowed to act) as though they are more important than others. Some are driven by the sales department. Some by operations. Some by singularly charismatic, dominant individuals.

But in order for a team to feel and *perform* like a team, it's vital to develop a culture where people understand why 'what they do' is vital to the organization and one in which no one department or team consciously or subconsciously believes that they are more important than the others.

- Don't pit people against one another or create power silos. Nip negative behaviors such as hoarding power, information or contacts in the bud. And conversely, make it absolutely safe for people to share information, power, contacts and even customers by behaving with integrity yourself, and insisting that all employees do the same.

4. Great teams recruit strategically. They go after the best players for each position; people who are not only great at what they do, but people whose strengths, personality (on and off the field) and abilities complement their style of play, work to fulfill their game plan, enhance and complement the strengths of other players and ultimately will help to generate not only immediate "wins" but also to build the team for the future.

- When hiring, remember that you are not just looking for superstars, you are looking for individuals who will fit in well with the employee culture that you have (or the one you want to develop).

- If you want to have a positive workplace, you must hire people who are positively charged.

  If you want to grow your business, you must hire people who can embrace change, welcome the suggestions and ideas of others and understand the concept of continuous improvement.

If you want to deliver exceptional customer experiences, you must hire people who are positive, patient, knowledgeable, good at problem solving, can think on their feet, who don't take criticism personally and who absolutely live to make the lives of others better.

- Hire for personality and attitude as well as abilities and experience. Make sure that not only your screening and interview processes but also your reference checks include questions which will help you determine whether the individual will be a good fit relative to other employees, whether they will add skills and abilities that you strategically desire, and whether they are individuals who can help you achieve not only short term "wins" but also fit in to how you plan to grow or change your business in the future.

5. Great teams are committed to continuous improvement which they achieve by running drills, training, education and good old practice, practice, practice.

Never satisfied with "good enough" or how good they were last season or during the last game, great teams constantly analyze their own performance to identify areas where they can improve, and then set out to do so. Great players work out regularly to stay in shape and strategically to get stronger and faster.

Great players don't just study the game plan, they completely internalize it. They learn every play so that, if called upon, they can do anything they are called upon to do to the absolute best of their ability.

- For many businesses, especially small businesses, this is an area which is often shelved for some time in the future when you believe that you will have "free time" to develop a plan for improvement.

  In many businesses, employees are putting in "good enough" performances because there are no reasons or incentives for them to go above and beyond the call of duty. They don't see a career path. Opportunities for development and advancement are not put in front of them (or encouraged). Mentoring and cross-training— practicing new skills—is non-existent.

- Have you created a climate of continuous improvement, or is "good enough" good enough at your business? Do you incentivize, reward or acknowledge ideas for improving sales, reducing costs, increasing efficiencies and other process improvements? Do you make it safe for people to make suggestions and share ideas relative to their own roles and even ideas that might impact the roles of others?

- Do you encourage or support continuing education and training? Do you even have a training plan? How about a job mentoring or employee development program?

- How often do you even analyze the 'play' of your team to look for areas which can be improved? Do you conduct employee and customer surveys? Do you encourage and facilitate customer or employee feedback in any way? Do you act on ideas and complaints? Do you report results?

6. Great teams take time to reassess and adjust their game plan mid-season or even mid-game, and they do so for many reasons. They may have lost key players due to injury or trades. They may have lost one or more coaches, or even fired them for poor performance. Or what they are doing may simply not be working.

- Part of your planning process should include incremental measurements; points in time when you will step back and analyze whether the tactics you are employing are working. You (and all the members of your team) must be able and willing to make needed adjustments to your game plan. You must be open to change.

- Create a culture where managers and employees feel safe; safe to make suggestions and where criticisms are given and taken constructively (rather than personally). It's not easy to develop this type of climate, and it starts at the top. Furthermore, it is a climate to which all of the leaders in your organization should be held accountable.

- This is not a culture you will develop by accident. 'Fight or flight' is often human nature when it comes to confrontation and criticism. Creating a culture where it is safe for the people within it to operate, make and receive suggestions and implement needed change is something you will only achieve when it's an authentic part of who you are as the leader of your business and the steps you take strategically to nurture it.

7. Great teams listen to experts on and off the field. Great teams don't just have one great coach, or even a great coach plus a great offensive and defensive coordinator. Great teams have experts on and off the field and in the booth, people who have a different perspective of things because of where they are sitting, who can be tapped for advice and insight.

- This might be scary for you, because top down, dictatorial leadership can seem easier. It may even give you the illusion of having control—but control is not the way to build a great team. To build a great team, all of the leaders and influencers within your business need to be developed, and need to feel (and should be) valued and heard.

- To build a great team, you need to tap the advice and insights of people who are watching your game from a different perspective. No man is an island, and great leaders seek out mentors, peers and consultants who can provide them with real time feedback on their own performance as well as that of their team.

8. Great teams work multiple channels of public relations, and they do so strategically. Great teams do not just release news, updates and other information to the public, they do so strategically. They have people assigned to address requests from the press and to communicate with the general public via web, social media and other online avenues.

Great teams do not release information that would give competitors an edge; they play things close to the vest when it's important to do so. However, they also have a plan for damage control when it comes to acknowledging problems and telling the public what they are going to do to rectify them.

On the other hand, great teams also know how to share information of human interest to garner fan affection and sympathy. How many times have you watched a game on television and heard one or more stories about a player's rise from poverty or how they overcame an illness or faced a personal tragedy?

And great teams make not only their coaches but their star players available to the public—and they also prep and train them to help them better present themselves in a positive light in the public eye.

- Develop a communications schedule to support short and long term goals and objectives (which, of course, assumes that you have some type of written plan and specific sales, customer acquisition and retention and other goals). Once you have a basic schedule, use it strategically to develop customer engagement, provide education about your products and services and support current and future initiatives.

- Part of communicating strategically is staying on point. This does not mean that you only talk about your company, it means that even when sharing outside ideas and resources in order to build your reputation as an expert resource for your audience, everything that you share in outbound communications (email, social media, etc.) relates to topics your audience would logically connect you or your business with. Make sense?

- Invest in communications training for yourself and your staff. You cannot assume that all of your staff possess an intrinsic ability to communicate both effectively and appropriately. You might not even feel that these are your strong points.

  Write scripts. Train staff. Practice. Have a second pair of eyes review updates that will be posted to social media as well as blog posts, press releases, outbound correspondence, memos that will be added to invoices or other customer forms and even to internal memos (which could negatively impact your staff, and in turn, the morale of your workplace).

Sounds like a lot of work, doesn't it? Great teams take the time to do it right, the first time. Think about that NFL team, where mistakes could be not only costly but devastating, resulting in team losses, season destruction or personnel changes. *With so much at stake, isn't the extra effort and training worth it?*

- Last, but certainly not least: Share the story of your business and human interest stories about your team members.

- Get involved in your community and talk about that, too. Champion local schools and charitable causes. Lead 'buy local' campaigns that keep dollars in your community.

- Give people reasons to connect with you and your business emotionally and to identify themselves with your business and your brand.

- Give people reasons to believe that when they align themselves with your business through loyalty and referrals, they are part of something good, part of something truly special.

9. Great teams cultivate adoration—nay, rabid enthusiasm—from among their fans. They position themselves to appeal to the types of fans they most desire. They know who their most important and influential fans are.

They establish emotional connections and develop loyalty that does just last for a season, but a lifetime; loyalty that is even passed on to the next generation.

Their fans are not only willing to spend money to attend a game or order up a season's worth via cable or satellite TV, but who are willing to purchase all kinds of extra merchandise for apparel or their homes in order to show that they are "part" of the team.

- If you are struggling just to get people in the door to begin with or with finding ways to get them to return a second time, thinking about how you could develop this type of loyalty might seem light years away from where you are right now. But here is what I say: If they can do it, you can do it—because it can be done.

- The way to begin is to focus on engagement and use customer relationship management techniques to move prospects to customer status and move customers through the customer life cycle to the next level of relationship.

10. The owners of great teams invest in the future and in adding the best players and coaches to their rosters. And it's not just that they go after "the best" players or coaches; there are many great players and coaches they would not want on their team because, although they are superstars, they would not be a good fit. They spend the money necessary to attract top players to their team who are not only experts or highly skilled at certain things, but they also go after great players strategically; they want those who represent a good fit for their company, other team members and for the long term as well as short term.

The owners of great teams are **always** investing toward the future.

- What about you? Do you hire strategically? Do you wait for the right person or fill positions with 'warm bodies?' Do you consider the impact to other team members? Do you consider personality type? Do you prepare team members to welcome a new player that might be a superstar (and therefore represent a threat to existing team members or become the basis for jealousy and insecurity on the part of team members)?

- Remember that long range plan? How are you investing for the future? Train and mentor team members to prepare for growth as well as enable it. Keep your team in the know when it comes to your vision for the future and the route you will take to get there. Ensure that people understand that they are important to you and that you value them, and that you are also interested in helping them to develop personally and professionally. Build an employee culture that is safe and welcoming for all team members and help those prone to jealousy or insecurity to change (or help them to realize that they might be happier somewhere else).

  And ultimately, remember that your responsibility is not only to the individuals who work for you, but that you are responsible to your customers and your business, and what is best for the team as a whole.

- Part of thinking about the future and investing in it may require that you have difficult conversations with team members who may no longer be as invested in their role as they were when they first started, who may not be supportive of how you want to grow your company, or who regularly negatively impact your employee culture in some way. Employer loyalty is not a valid excuse for retaining employees who negatively impact your business, customers or their co-workers.

  Remember that the choice to support the initiatives, goals and objectives of your business, the choice to live out the mission and vision of the company *rests with each individual employee.* If they cannot or will not choose to align themselves with the mission and vision of your organization, should they be part of your team?

11. Great coaches know how to motivate and inspire players to perform even better than they believed they could. And great coaches know which players to put in, when, and they call the right plays. Great coaches inspire confidence and trust in their players and from their assistant coaches and support staff. And on great teams, players have trust and faith in one another.

- While we often think that emotion has no place in the workplace, have you ever watched what happens on the field and on the sidelines during a game? Coaches and players get fired up, get excited, celebrate big plays, turnovers and scores. They wave their arms to fire up the crowd. Thousands and thousands of people, all excited about the same thing in the same place at the same time.

This occurs as a result of *emotional connection*, not logic.

- Cultivate an employee culture of trust. Do what you say you will do and insist that all staff members do so, as well. Hold people accountable. Leave no room in your company for backbiting, gossip or individuals who choose to undermine the efforts of others or even corporate initiatives.

- Don't throw people under the bus publicly. Part of being a great leader means that you will, occasionally, be the one who takes a hit because one of your employees makes a mistake.

  Taking a hit for a subordinate or co-worker may be one of the most powerful signals you can send to your whole team that you have their backs, always.

12. Great teams start out by playing to win, and keep on playing to win. Great teams don't get complacent and never seem to tire. They play every minute of every game until the final buzzer sounds. They don't assume that any lead is safe. They don't abandon the strategies and tactics that put them in the lead. Great teams keep on keeping on!

- What about you? Have you relaxed your vigilance when it comes to competitors? Have you let programs lapse or failed to measure or follow up on initiatives?

- Continue to execute the strategies and tactics which are bringing your business desired results, a measure of stability and maybe even competitive advantage. Analyze the competition for weaknesses which might be indicative of areas where you can gain ground. Maintain a mindset where you constantly scanning the field, thinking strategically and taking calculated risks in order to gain ground. Play to your strengths and bring great players to your team who can help 'carry the ball' even further.

13. Great teams reward and acknowledge great performances and loyalty. Great performances are rewarded with game balls, sideline celebrations and most valuable player awards for games and even whole seasons.

Great players who perform at a consistently high level and prove themselves loyal over time have jerseys retired, get streets named after them and are inducted to team and even industry halls of fame.

Not a single game passes by where extraordinary individual performances resulting in contributions to the team are not recognized, acknowledged and rewarded.

- What an incredible model! Who have you acknowledged or thanked today? For that matter, when was the last time someone put in an acknowledgement-worthy performance in your business? If you cannot think of one, you are either not paying attention or it's (past) time to seriously evaluate and improve your employee culture.

14. Great teams are known for something. No two teams are alike in specialty, mix of players, strategy or playbooks. No two teams look alike; in fact, teams go to great lengths to differentiate their visual brand identity.

- Great companies are known for something specific. They are known for their specialties. Their founders. Their stories. Their charitable and public contributions.

What is your business known *for*?

- The path to success is not to be a copycat. Rather, the path to greatness is about identifying and choosing skills and specialties that will make your company different from the competition.

  It's about identifying niche markets and finding where opportunity exists—looking for the gaps—and providing solutions there.

  It's about thinking for the future and developing products and services that will meet emerging customer needs and wants. You are cultivating and educating prospects and customers. Set yourself apart!

14 Characteristics of Great Teams.

Easy to write, not so easy to live up to—but start, today.

Try today and try again tomorrow.

Get your team on board; but remember, you have to believe in these things yourself, and endeavor to model them with authenticity to your team, before they will be willing to reciprocate—especially if there is a history where these traits were not part of your value system.

Playing to win

If you watch a lot of football like I do, it's not uncommon to watch your favorite team gain an edge over their opponent and get a small lead; and then, with time left on the clock, for reasons I will never understand, your team abandons the strategy which helped them get the lead to begin with (which usually involved assertive play and calculated risk taking on both offense and defense) and starts playing "not to lose," hoping to run out the clock before the other team can overtake their lead.

When they—or you—play "not to lose," what invariably happens is that your competitor will have the opportunity to take advantage of your less aggressive, "safe" approach.

They stop you on offense, because you are trying to keep the ball on the ground and you fail to make a needed first down. And once they get the ball back, they march right down the field and into scoring range because your defense isn't working to force turnovers and they aren't taking calculated risks in order to put extra players in anticipation of what the next play might be.

It's true for business, not just football.

You worked hard to get your business established; you took calculated risks and tried things you had not tried before in order to gain an edge.

But after you have gained some ground, you became so afraid to lose your position that you started playing "not to lose" instead of playing to win. For instance,

- You acquired a few hundred (or even thousand) fans on Facebook or Twitter but you are so afraid of one or two of them "unliking" your page that you are afraid to post things that will provoke and connect with people emotionally.

  You are afraid to speak passionately on social media. Your posts are about as exciting as a bowl of oatmeal (which, incidentally, is how they are making your brand look, as well).

  You are afraid that if you post more than once a day someone will get annoyed and stop reading your posts. So you are not playing to win on social media, you are playing "not to lose."

- Instead of making your business—and your customer experience—truly unique, you are playing it safe by keeping things as generic as possible. And so once the customer walks out, there is *nothing* memorable to make them want to come back and nothing that makes them want to tell their friends about you.

- Instead of adding value and changing your lineup— taking a few calculated risks in order to compete in the new economy—you are holding on to the way you have always done things. You are more focused on not losing one or two customers than you are on gaining new ones by making changes you need to make within your business.

- Instead of engaging with your customers through communications, you are so worried that someone might unsubscribe from your emailing list if you actually email them that you never do it at all; or at most, you send one or two one-and-done offers and a holiday greeting each year.

Or even worse, maybe you don't have a playbook at all, and everything that you are doing is being done as a one-and-done, because there is no short or long term strategy in play.

There is still plenty of time on the clock: are playing not to lose? Or playing to win?

Little White Marketing Lie #9:

"Employee culture has nothing to do with marketing."

Comedian Henny Youngman once cracked, "I told my doctor that I broke my leg in two places. He told me to stop going to those places."

It's a ridiculous concept; that we would return time and time again to a place where we know we are going to get hurt, but in business, *we do it all the time.*

You can spot a broken leg via x-ray (and sometimes even without one); but the injuries I am talking about do not show up to the naked eye, which may be why we neither treat nor work to prevent them.

What am I talking about?

We constantly allow individuals within our businesses to 'injure' or even 'kill' initiatives, employee morale, customer relations and more.

Under the auspices of loyalty to employees or the value we perceive they bring to the business, we overlook, make excuses for, tolerate and even facilitate cynicism, narcissism, gossip, turf wars and negativism from certain employees.

You know who I am talking about — employees who regularly pooh-pooh your marketing and event ideas, who belittle, cut down and minimize the accomplishments of others out of envy, who flaunt their disdain for rules by ignoring the standards you try to set for employees in the areas of appearance, timeliness, productivity, retail sales, etc.

If there were such a ridiculous place in your life (like, say a grocery store) where you knew you would always receive an injury, how often would you go there?

Assuming you would not subject *yourself* to needless injury:
why would you subject your business to it
and why do you subject your employees to it?

How many times can you afford to allow any employee to injure coworkers, harm your business or do damage to your customer relationships?

Were you to do a cost-analysis of this type of behavior, you would likely find that the damage these individuals are doing to your business, to their co-workers, and to your customer-relations far outweighs the (real or perceived) value you believe they bring to your business.

Employer loyalty is wonderful; but is it fair to your business or your other employees when you extend loyalty to individuals who *do not* return that loyalty through their actions by way of supporting of your initiatives, their co-workers and in productivity and professional growth?

Not only is it unfair to you and to your business, it is also unfair for the other individuals who have to work with them, and, ultimately, it is *extremely unfair* to expect your customers to extend loyalty to you when the services and care you provide for them are *compromised* by these individuals.

And I will guarantee you that no matter where in your organization these negative individuals are harbored (and you know who they are), they *are* compromising the customer experience, whether they are doing so directly or indirectly.

But (you say) we are talking about people.

People are not all good or all bad; you believe that some of them have irreplaceable skills or that among their clientele are long-time patrons your business cannot afford to lose.

Yes, we are talking about people; and yes, highly flawed people are sometimes also incredibly talented—but that still doesn't outweigh the negative impact they have on your business.

Let me put it another way.

Let's say you have a friend that cooks a wonderful lunch, the best lunch you have ever had. But every time you go there for lunch, you are assured of receiving a kick to the chin or a slap in the face.

How often would you want to lunch there, no matter how spectacular the food?

This is **exactly** how it feels for other employees when they are the target of belittling comments or gossip from other employees.

This is **exactly** how it feels for customers when they are mistreated while at your business or on the phone with that one bad apple on your customer service team.

This is **exactly** how you probably feel when you go into a staff meeting excited about a new idea, only to have the negative person on your staff blow it all to pieces.

My mom, who has nearly four decades of professional management experience, often said to me, "Reward behavior you want more of."

By rewarding those who exhibit defiance, discourteous behavior, disdain or negativity, you are _ensuring_ that you will receive more of the same behavior.

You are also demonstrating to other employees that these techniques work. You discouraging employees who are excited about their work and your business and you are also showing those who may have similar negative inclinations that this behavior is acceptable and effective.

Am I suggesting a "slash and burn" employment policy?

No.

But I am suggesting that those individuals who cannot be persuaded to bring a spirit of positive support (or at least neutrality!) to the workplace, who will not endorse your policies and standards, or who regularly hurt other employees or even offend clients themselves, are _in the wrong place._

First, they are in the wrong place **on the inside.**

They should be in a profession and in a business that they can endorse intellectually and philosophically.

They should be excited about their work and should be just as enthusiastic to try a new marketing technique or hold a new event as they are to do something new that they personally enjoy.

They should be able to extend (sincere) congratulations and encouragement to their co-workers in the same way that they would want to be supported.

They should be in a place where they are comfortable adhering to standards of dress, conduct, and interpersonal communications.

If they cannot do these things, **then they are in the wrong place on the outside**, and they may need to find another organization in which to work.

Your job, as a manager of people is to encourage them either to discover whether they can change 'where they are' on the inside, or to change where they are on the outside (and seek other employment).

Your obligation to sustain and grow your business, and to protect and develop all of your employees outweighs the obligation you believe you have to retain an employee who is in the wrong place on the inside.

CHAPTER BONUS:

3 Characteristics of a Real Team
(and a lesson from the marching band)

In 2011, a Harvard Business Review's 'Management Tip of the Day' post noted three characteristics of real teams. They pointed out that the word "team," as used in business today, has lost its true meaning.

To be rightly called a team, and to maximize their potential, they say a group must be characterized by all three of these things:

- a meaningful and common purpose,
- adaptable skills, *and*
- mutual accountability.

No secret to you by now, I believe that the employee culture of your business has everything to do with marketing and with the potential for success of your business.

Accountability (and, by extension, consequences) must be part of your approach to leadership if you want to build a successful business.

Many business owners have become so used to opposition when it comes to making even the most necessary and smallest of changes, that they often give up on a good idea if its implementation or execution requires the buy in of certain employees.

I know that sometimes it seems *almost impossible* to make even the *smallest changes* when it necessitates the cooperation of your team.

In fact, sometimes it feels like your employees actually *want* new ideas to fail, even if it means less success for themselves and their co-workers, as well as your business.

Your employees—those individuals who would most directly benefit in the short and long term by helping to make your business more successful—should be the **most enthusiastic** supporters of process changes and initiatives designed to make customers more happy or attract new customers to your business.

So why doesn't it always work that way?

As human beings, we all bring our own ideas, prejudices, experiences, likes and dislikes into the employee group. Just because someone joins your team, it does not necessarily mean that they all do so with the same level of commitment and enthusiasm that you desire or even demonstrate.

And even if someone joins your team with a high level of enthusiasm and energy for business-building activities, it still doesn't ensure that they will agree with your ideas on how to build clientele or even who your "ideal clients" should be relative to marketing activities.

And even if they do, it still does not mean they will agree with the environment and "feel" that you want all of your clients to experience in your business.

What does all of this have to do with employee culture? Everything.

Your employee culture is a reflection of the sum total values, beliefs, attitudes, ideas, experiences, assumptions and behaviors shared by your staff.

And this culture is reflected back to your clients in *every area* of your business.

If your employee culture is characterized by attitudes that are negative, lazy or careless, unmotivated or cynical, it is because those traits are present to some extent in one or more of your staff, and it is because these negative traits *are allowed* to dominate and influence daily operations.

To be clear, I am saying that if your employee culture is defined by one or more of these negative traits, it is because *you*, as the leader of your business, are allowing them to remain.

It all comes down to choice.

Remember those three team characteristics? If they don't characterize your team, then either you have not requested that your team members <u>choose</u> to embrace a meaningful, common purpose or you have <u>chosen</u> to **not** hold them accountable for the choices they are making instead.

Does this mean that you should only hire and retain employees who think exactly like you? Not at all. It is the variety of experiences, talents, skills and interests—the differences within us as people, when shared—that leads to higher levels of creativity, imagination, resourcefulness, abilities and strengths.

But your business will grow and thrive only to the extent that these strengths, passions and creativity can be harnessed to pull toward the same goals; and when this occurs in a spirit of positive energy and optimism rather than predominant negativity.

Have you ever seen a marching band in action on the field during the halftime period at a football game?

You might see a hundred or more people, all working together to play the same song.

By mutual agreement, all of them use their individual strengths, abilities and play different instruments in order to deliver a performance for the audience.

Every step they take is even *choreographed* specifically to further engage and entertain the audience visually, even beyond the music.

Together, they create a visual, changing design that, like the music, is made up of completely individual routes and roles, *purposefully designed* and choreographed to create a visual whole made up of the sum of all its parts.

Each member has different skills and strengths, and many are skilled soloists in their own right as musicians and/or even as dancers.

But as band members they come together with an understanding that the good of the whole organization is greater than the glory of any one individual.

They voluntarily submit to the choices of their band director, choreographer and other unit leaders, knowing that it is only by working together that the organization will be successful; they equate their own success to that of the band as a whole.

They agree—they <u>choose</u>, if you will—to pool their strengths, skills and abilities in order to achieve a group goal—to perform the same song, to the same beat, as directed by the band leader, in order to please their clients—the audience.

School band members know that they will only be playing together for a short time, maybe even only for one year; yet they still come to this agreement and shared goal and they work at perfecting it, nearly every day.

In the case of your business, where some of you may work together for decades, is not it even more important for you to agree to work together toward the shared goals of attracting and pleasing your clients? Of meeting your customer's needs and making them feel that they are, in fact, vitally important to your business?

How does your team stack up to these three characteristics of real teams? How do they stack up against a student marching band? And what are you doing to build a true team within your business?

Little White Marketing Lie #10:

"What's in the past is in the past."

Marketing Caution:
Objects in mirror are closer than they appear

Last summer our family vacation included a road-trip day, driving from Fond du Lac, Wisconsin to just north of Battle Creek, Michigan. Wanting to get a blog post written on the drive, I decided to peruse roadside advertising for some marketing inspiration.

What I got was a series of ho-hum, cliché billboards for various restaurants, sales, and the like; I thought about the futility some companies go to when they think they have come up with a catchy tagline—it's such an expensive endeavor, and in most cases, no one will remember them.

Why not?

It takes an incredible amount of market advertising in order to state, restate and keep restating any tagline (or logo, for that matter) so that it becomes ingrained in the minds of consumers.

And ultimately, as I said in the bonus section of chapter one, words are just words until someone comes along and gives them meaning. Your tagline and logo simply will not become ingrained in the minds of your customers until you put strong, truly exceptional customer experiences behind them.

A bit dejected at the wastefulness of a lot of the marketing efforts I saw alongside the road, I caught site of the side mirror. Unlike the series of forgettable billboards I had been watching fly by, my mirror featured a 'tagline' that *is* memorable, and one we've all heard before, as it warned:

Objects in mirror are closer than they appear.

A-ha, I thought, that is very true in life as well as on the road.

Things we were not watching out for—competitors, technology, unhappy people we thought were in our past, and other things can catch up to us, overtake us, or even run us off the road if we are not paying attention.

From a marketing standpoint, you should check your rear-view mirrors often for these three things that are likely much, much closer than they appear, and which can run you off the road:

1- The Competition

- When was the last time you took note of what your direct and indirect competitors are doing?

- Is there a new business in town?

- Is new technology available to your industry?

- Is there a substitute product or service offering that could make what you have to offer obsolete or overpriced?

- Who among your competitors is doing 'what you do' better than you? More efficiently? More inexpensively?

And just like on the road, don't just watch what the competitor right behind you is doing; watch out for speedsters who might just be coming up fast in the lane beside you.

2—Dissatisfied Customers

You have probably heard this before: It's not necessarily a problem that will result in a lost customer; it's how you handle the problem.

That customer who left yesterday in a huff because your clerk was rude, distracted or un-knowledgeable about your products or services? Today they are calling you, sending you an e-mail or writing you a letter to tell you that you failed to satisfy.

(That is, *if you are lucky* they are contacting you to complain; if not, they are already on Facebook telling all their friends and the whole world about how bad your business is.)

You thought you left the problem behind when the customer walked out the door, but those bad reviews are going to be much, much closer than they appear, and they will result in lost business and lost sales.

Responding to customer complaints as quickly as possible will help to minimize damage to your reputation and bad reviews online. If you messed up, say so, and make it right.

Even if your business did nothing wrong, you should still acknowledge the complainant's feelings and experience as legitimate (their perception is, after all, their reality) and do what you can to provide them with new, more positive experiences.

3—Problem Employees

So you sat down with the employee who caused the dissatisfaction noted in point #2 above, and now you believe that the problem is in the past. But if this employee has a history of providing poor customer experiences or if your communication was not clear to them, you stand a good chance of continued problems.

A point I have made in all of my books, including 365 Days of Marketing: employer loyalty is misplaced when it is bestowed equally on top performers and conscientious, customer-service minded staff as it is on individuals who provide poor customer service, who negatively impact morale in your organization, who are cynical or even subversive when it comes to your programs and initiatives or who otherwise negatively impact your organization.

As you are cruising down the proverbial business road, don't forget to check those rear-view mirrors for these things that could come back to run you off the road!

Little White Marketing Lie #11:

"There's no room for emotion in the workplace."

Recently a small business owner claimed to me that they have—and insist on—a "drama free" work environment. While I am not entirely sure what he meant, since as human beings it is inevitable that problems—and sometimes dramatic problems—come into our lives and cannot help but affect our ability to perform, our attitude, or demeanor and energy level in the workplace, I took it to mean that they fostered a culture free of unnecessary drama that can be caused by destructive behaviors like complaining, gossip, power struggles and the like.

How many times have you heard that emotion has no place in the workplace? As I pondered the idea and thought about how often we think that every problem can be solved if we can only apply enough logic and keep our emotions out of the equation, I realized that it just is not true.

And yet, so often we avoid any and all displays of emotion, even in front of our co-workers, and especially in front of our customers. For many reasons.

When we see other people in the throes of strong emotions, it often makes us uncomfortable, as it evokes an emotional response within us or triggers memories of problems or people who have caused us to experience strong emotions in the past. We don't always know how to deal with our own emotion in the workplace—let alone those of others. And some people suffer from the misconception that they are too professional—too mature—to display emotion in the workplace.

While it's true that we need to apply heaping portions of logic when it comes to solving problems in our business, and while it's true that we should strive to keep negative behaviors our of our workplaces which can cause unnecessary drama, one look at some of the most successful organizations in the world should give you a different perspective when it comes to emotion in the workplace.

Companies like Apple, Starbucks and Coca-Cola know this; they thrive because they have mastered the art of triggering and using emotion in order to create hoards of rabidly loyal fans, inside as well as outside of their organizations.

And if you spend any time around sports, you will realize just how natural it is for us, as human beings, to display even very strong and extreme emotions. You will see how great teams purposefully set out to evoke emotions, and in the process, create life-long, loyal and even multi-generational faithful fans.

And it's not just their fans (or customers). On great teams, players channel their emotions not into meaningless braggadocio, but into desired results on the field of play. The best players talk with their actions on the field.

And perhaps most important to point out, the members of great teams are themselves bonded through emotional connection, not just professional skill. If you have ever observed a favorite team with a rogue player who evokes negative responses from team-mates, you have also discovered that, no matter how skilled and talented players are, if they do not form emotional bonds with one another, inevitably the success of their team is negatively affected.

Without emotional bonding between teammates, teams simply cannot perform at their optimum levels.

So I pose this to you in answer to this little white marketing lie: Loyalty is not related to logic, it's related almost entirely to emotion.

And you cannot solve an emotional problem with a purely logical approach.

Logically, we would always shop for the best value for any item we want to buy. But once a business has successfully established and reinforced our satisfaction (this is an emotion, this is the way we *feel* that a company has exceeded our expectations) then, and only then, do they court our loyalty. Then and only then do they have a chance to win our loyalty in a way that transcends the lure of lower prices, better value or even better products offered by competitors.

Do you want your employees to be able to evoke emotion in the form of customer satisfaction?

The only way to stimulate this type of emotional satisfaction lies within the culture of your business. Your employees must feel emotionally invested in and identify with the brand of your business themselves.

Your staff must not only believe in the professional skill of their co-workers, but they must also be bonded to one another. They must be bonded emotionally with one another and with you as the leader of your business to develop this type of customer-satisfaction producing investment.

For initiatives to succeed, staff must also trust in the guidance of their "coach" (that is you) and believe in the wisdom of the "plays" that you are calling.

Belief and trust are emotional responses. They are triggered not only by the logical analysis of the guidance or play called by the coach, but they are emotions which are also affected based on their history with you and your business. They are affected by the extent to which employees believe their teammates and coaches have their backs, especially if they are going to go beyond the call of duty when it comes to courting customer satisfaction.

They are emotions based on the belief that both their coach and all of their co-workers will also do their own jobs well and that everyone on the team can be counted on to work for the progress and success of the team. Why?

Let me ask you this: **If your employees cannot trust one another** because the culture of your business is characterized by struggles for power, back-biting, criticism, complaints, envy, gossip or other negative, initiative-crushing traits, **why on earth would you expect your staff to want to identify themselves with the brand of your business or commit themselves to helping your business succeed?**

The livelihood and financial success (not to mention the potential for raises and bonuses) for all your employees rests on the ability of your business to identify and attract customers and for your business to create customer loyalty and satisfaction—yes?

And yet in most businesses, despite the financial incentive, fewer than a third of employees *feel* (emotionally) engaged with or self-identify with your business.

Logically, employees should be busting their butts to get your customers more emotionally connected with your business. But they are not.

And since they *are not*, you have to ask yourself, what is missing (or present) within the culture of your business that is failing to motivate your employees—who *logically* should be doing everything they can to work for business success that could translate into more financial reward for themselves. What is it about your business that is failing to attract and engage your employees *emotionally?*

To develop customer loyalty or employee fidelity, you must work logically, strategically and authentically within the realm of emotions to:

- cause people to view themselves as a connected to your business (and to you, as its leader)

- go beyond logical reasons; you must realize that loyalty is an emotional response

- garner the faith of others based on history and trust in the promises that you make relative to what customers or employees can expect to be true of all of their experiences with you and your business

Only by understanding the role that emotions play relative to employee or customer loyalty will you be able to create the type of emotional connection needed to cause employees to go beyond the call of duty (and in turn to garner customer loyalty) on behalf of the team as a whole. And only by building an employee culture characterized by trust, honesty and a sense of shared destiny will this occur.

More lessons from great teams when it comes to using emotions to build strong bonds with employees and customers:

- Set aside time in the "locker room" with employees in the form of meetings, training, continuing education, and private, one on one coaching when needed

- Develop individual plans for training and a career path for employees

- Give people opportunities to work and grow in their areas of their passions

- Review, rehearse and modify the game plan and ensure that all employees know the plan for the short and the long term

- Ensure that every employee understands their role and how they can most help the team

- Reward outstanding individual contributions and MVPs (most valuable players); just like the pros, make acknowledging and thanking employees part of your *daily* routine

- "Huddle up" at important moments or when new plays need to be called in order to take advantage of opportunities or gain ground on competitors

- Work the crowd; fan the flames of emotion following big positive plays and make your customers feel appreciated, as though they, themselves, are to be acknowledged as important contributors for successes

CHAPTER BONUS:

The view from under the bus

Good morning, I have been elected to speak to you on behalf of the group—those of us you have thrown under the bus, in the course of running your business, managing your team or otherwise trying to control the tiny little bit of commercial territory you have been allotted.

You said that you wanted us on board, and at first, we believed you.

We wanted it to be true.

We were excited about the trip and we thought that we understood the route we'd take to reach our destination.

But somehow we did not make it on board. We ended up under the bus, and now, covered in tread marks, I've been deputed to say:

Ouch.

Maybe you did not realize we were not on board.

Maybe you shut the door before we boarded. You put us in a dead end job. You ignored our ideas. You put us in our place and told us to just "do our jobs."

And when we did do our jobs, maybe you failed to notice. You failed to show any sign of gratitude or appreciation.

You made us feel as though you believe we exist to fulfill your ends, and as though the privilege of doing so should be reward enough.

Maybe you had good intentions but failed to deliver with employee development and training. Maybe you just did not train us at all.

Maybe, since you evidently believe that our jobs are not as important as yours, you made us feel like interchangeable, expendable tools. Maybe you were threatened by our enthusiasm and so chose to protect your own position by hoarding information and depriving us of opportunities to contribute in more meaningful ways.

Maybe you confined us to particularly unrewarding tasks, leaving us bored and deprived of any spark of creative renewal. You painted a picture of opportunity then failed to engage us, at all.

Or maybe, for your own reasons, you actually went ahead and shoved us directly under the wheels of your bus.

You blamed us when things went wrong. You did not stand up for us when co-workers or customers came after us. You took credit for our work. You made sure we knew that we could never, ever truly please you. You couched your compliments in criticisms. You made us feel like enthusiasm is a mockable quality.

For one reason or another, here we are, under the bus.

Well, let me tell you something: It's quite a view we have from down here.

If we look down, we face the prospect (pun intended) of being dragged along the pavement, with a close-up view of the road and all its hazards.

But when we look up, we see everything.

We know exactly how your bus works. We see all of the dirty, grimy, greasy and oily working parts. We know what's broken and we know what else is about to break. You might be able to talk a good game to people on the outside, or even other people in the bus; but we know better. You are not fooling us, not one little bit.

What's more, most of us have probably tried to tell you, more than once, about the problems, flaws, broken and about-to-break things that we've seen. You did not do anything about them, or you did not listen or worst of all, you told us to shut up, ignore it and "get back to work."

Eventually you are going to lose us completely—and this might be painful for one or even for both of us.

At some point, you might even realize that you lost a truly vital part of your 'engine,' something necessary to customer comfort or care—not to mention the deep pools of untapped skills and devotion that could have been at your disposal, had your promises matched up to the reality of our experience with you.

Or maybe you don't really care about what your customers, employees and coworkers experience during their ride at all, so long as you collect your fares.

If that is true, let me share one last word of collective warning from all those of us under here: Eventually someone will come along who'll offer a better ride to your customers and your employees, and you will find yourself broken down on the side of the highway, wondering what went wrong.

Do you know what this has to do with marketing? Only everything.

Your business is not the products or services you sell or the building or website from which you do so. Your business is made up of people. Real people. With feelings, ambitions, dreams, needs and wants—on the inside and out.

On the outside, these people are your customers, prospects, vendors, investors and other stakeholders. Given their roles and how important you perceive them to be to your business, it's likely that you listen to them more than you do to those "people" who make up your business from the inside: Your employees and co-workers.

It's ironic that once you get someone on the inside you stop considering their opinions. Because who has more vested interest in the success of your business than your employees— the people whose livelihood and future depend upon it? I'll tell you: no one.

Your customers might say they "love you" but they will get along just fine without you. It might hurt your vendors if you went away but they will find new relationships, too. Your employees are the ones with the most at stake. Your employees are the people closest to the problems. Your employees are the people most capable of coming up with creative solutions.

But it's really difficult for them to help you from under the bus.

Need more convincing?

Here is how important your employees are to the success of your business:

- Want more profit? Lost productivity due to actively disengaged employees costs the US economy $370 billion *every year*, and some of those billions are lost right in your business.

- Think customer service matters? 70% of engaged employees have a good understanding of how to meet customer needs; only 17% of non-engaged employees say the same.

- Like referrals? A mere 13% of disengaged employees refer others to their company, whereas 78% of engaged employees happily and readily do so.

- Like problem solvers? Only 3% of disengaged employees say their job brings out their creative side, vs. 59% of engaged employees.

- Think hiring is difficult and expensive? 75% of people don't leave their 'jobs,' they quit their bosses.

- Fewer than 1 in 3 employees worldwide *feel* 'engaged.'

- Companies with more engaged employees experience dramatically lower rates of turnover, absenteeism and even a 50% reduction in reportable incidents (a.k.a., workers comp). Do those things impact your bottom line?

- And even though 90% of business leaders say that employee engagement impacts their success, 75% of them have no—nada—zero –none—no engagement plan or strategy—at all.

SOURCE: 'Human Capital and Corporate Culture' at
http://www.thesocialworkplace.com/2011/08/08/social-knows-employee-engagement-statistics-august-2011-edition/

Now that I have your attention, what will you do about it?

Roll merrily along and wait for the whole thing to come off the wheels? Or will you take time now to make things right—or at least make them better!

You only have today and the time is now to make sure that all the people who could and should be most invested in the success of your business are in a position to feel engaged, satisfied and even happy as a result of the employment relationship with you. Now is the time for you to ask the hard questions and be open to the realization that maybe you don't have it all figured out, after all.

Now is the time for you to decide just where this bus is going to take all of its passengers, and set out to get there, together!

Little White Marketing Lie #12:

"Service professionals aren't sales people."

In *any* service profession, the key to success is client trust.

Because they think that it actually erodes client trust, many service professionals resist "selling" like the plague. They are afraid to sound like pushy, stereo-typical used car salesmen. They don't want to pressure their clients. Asking clients to purchase products makes them uncomfortable.

But I have news for you. As a service professional, your success depends not only on the skill with which you practice your craft, but it also depends on selling products.

Why?

You must build client trust to be successful. And you must sell retail products to build client trust.

Here is why:

Selling the right products to your clients is your responsibility; you may be the only person who will fully assess problems and know how to solve them.

Selling clients the right products gives them the tools they need to meet long-term goals.

- Selling products keeps you on the client's mind; when they use your products at home they will remember the advice and instructions you gave, and will watch for the benefits you predicted to materialize.

- Sending clients home with professional products will stimulate subconscious memories of how they felt catered to, relaxed, pampered, special and/or important while in your care.

- Products that perform as advertised and deliver on benefits give clients a reason to come to back to you for additional purchases.

- Selling products which perform as you said they would reinforces the client's confidence in your knowledge, expertise and ability. Prescription, accompanied by product or service performance, proves to your clients that you are the expert.

Convinced?

Now that you know why you should do it, are some ways you can make selling retail an organic part of your business, and which can take all the pain and fear out of the selling process for you:

- First and foremost: always and only make authentic recommendations. If you sell for your own benefit (rather than a client's genuine need) you will lose trust. Once lost, trust is difficult to regain.

- Use a visual take-away tool, like a prescription form, business card with an area to list recommendations, follow up e-mail or direct mail collateral or some other system, religiously, as part of each and every client consultation.

- Change your mind set. Making product recommendations is part of the service you provide. You have a professional obligation to tell clients about what you observe and how products and services can help.

- Don't talk about products; talk about problems and solutions, conditions and cures. Talk about the client's goals in relationship to the products they need.

- Talk in terms of the benefits to the client, not the virtue or 'newness' of any product. It's not that you have a great new product that does such-and-such, it's that your client needs a product because it provides certain specific, unique client benefits. *See the difference?*

- Put selling tools to work on your behalf. Merchandise, (focusing on client-centric benefits) from the inside-out. Website and blog posts, e-mail newsletters, postcards, social media status updates, posters on windows and walls, shelf and station talkers, point of sale displays, samples, 'try me' stations, bag stuffers, thank you notes or e-mails, prescription pads, recommendation cards and appointment reminders— at least 15 ways to introduce your clients to the products they need—without saying a word!

- Reformulate pricing to include products in the price of certain services or create bundled packages or series. That way, you are a hero— you are "giving" products to your clients or saving them money by combining products or services.

Little White Marketing Lie #13:

"Social media isn't critical to our marketing strategy."

Long gone are the days when taking out a yellow pages listing, an ad, sending a postcard or handing out a few flyers got the marketing job done.

You simply cannot afford to believe you don't need a social media marketing toolbox, one stuffed to the gills with hard-working tools that you will use just about every day.

Social media is now a full-fledged member of the marketing tactics family.
It's not a passing fad, it is here to stay.

Whether or not you have personal prejudices against Facebook, Twitter or any other online social network, you cannot afford to let your personal prejudices hold your business back.

It's high time for you to get in the social media game, if you haven't already. Social media costs little beyond time and effectively levels the playing field between businesses of all sizes.

And social media is critical to your SEO (search engine optimization) and SEM (search engine marketing) strategy. The more likes, retweets, +1s and other shares your online content receives, the better your business will do in online search results. The better you do in online search results, the more people that find your business. And the more people that find your business, the more new customers you attract and the more sales you make.

But don't just take my word for it. In 2011, a Social Media Examiner (www.socialmediaexaminer.com) report noted the 4 most popular and effective social media sites for business as Facebook, Twitter, LinkedIn and Blogging (in that order.) The Social Media Examiner report noted that:

> **Small businesses were <u>twice as likely</u> to find qualified leads and nearly <u>50% more likely</u> to see improved sales as a result of using social media than were their larger counterparts.**

Convinced? Here are the leading social networks you need to consider (as of right now) to be central components of your online marketing strategy:

1. Facebook. In 2011, 1 out of every 8 minutes spent online was spent on Facebook (Hubspot.com). As you read the list that follows, which is just a starting point for how you can use Facebook and other social media, ask yourself this question: What other aspect of your business gives you the opportunities to do what social media is providing?

Among other things, you can use Facebook to:

- engage people who already know about or already like your business
- share expert information
- make announcements
- solicit feedback
- use the voice and personality of your business to attract prospects
- post trivia about your community
- post status updates that include motivational quotes
- post links to human interest stories
- promote interest in your favorite charities and community organizations
- use giveaways and contests to spark engagement and get new followers
- help fill the books during slow hours
- stimulate event RSVPs
- interact with your most important clients

2. Twitter. Good news: Using Twitter for your business will not take a lot of time. Twitter status posts are like 140 character social media posts with A.D.D. Plus, many of the same things you will post on Facebook will simply be cross-posted to Twitter, although you need to keep that 140 character limit in mind.

You can also use Twitter to:

- provide links to content on your website and blog
- extend the reach and readership of your e-mail newsletter

- extend other social media posts farther and wider
- post motivational, amusing or provocative quotes (studies show that posts which are both interesting and amusing get the most retweets) that help to build your number of followers and which reinforce the perception that you are an expert

3. LinkedIn. LinkedIn took a while to develop to the point that it provided substantial value for its members. But once it found its niche, it really took off and now provides tangible value for business owners and professionals as a tool for networking and recruiting. Using LinkedIn will not take up too much time and you can cross post from your website, e-mail, blog and Facebook. Per the Social Media Examiner study, for B2B businesses, LinkedIn is the #1 tool for connecting with peers.

4. Blogging. For businesses, blogging is a valuable tool, one unmatched for providing your business with a voice and the means to reach out to prospects and customers with undiluted, detailed, branded messages.

A corporate blog is a type of website for your business (although not a substitute for a true corporate website) that gives you an unlimited amount of space to have your say. Use your blog to educate prospects and customers, talk about your industry, explain your technologies, make promises to customers about the benefits of doing business with you, and so much more.

And if you are an independent professional, blogging is a great way to build your reputation as an expert.

In both cases, as with other social networks, your blog is not the place to push in hard-sell style; instead, educate, build awareness and enhance your expert reputation.

Use Top 10 lists and "Did you know..." style posts to talk about new products, services, trends, fads, innovations, etc.

Tell people about the wonderful things that your business does within your community. Talk about how your business helps charities. Explain the ways in which your business is acting in social and environmentally responsible ways.

The following social media tools were *not* part of the 2011 Social Media Examiner report, and this brings up a good point:

Social media in general is a full-fledged member of marketing and one that you cannot afford to ignore. However, because of the nature of the internet, the rapid pace at which it develops and the ease with which it allows developers to bring new platforms to market, the social media marketing strategies and tactics you employ for your business need to be chosen based on their effectiveness relative to the goals of your business and you need to remember that your mix may change.

In fact, the tactics you use to achieve your marketing goals on social media, including the platforms you will use, need to be re-evaluated on a regular basis—probably more frequently than do other components of your overall marketing plan.

Case in point: Google+ was only talked about in whispers at the time of the report cited above; yet now, less than a year later, is considered a vital and non-negotiable "must" for every business' marketing strategy. Why? Because it's Google, and because of how they changed the game for content marketing and SEO with the launch of Google+.

5. Google+. Google+ both is and is not just another social network. It is a social network in the sense that you use it by connecting with other Google+ users who follow you (or whom you follow). It is more or less similar to some other platforms in that you share status updates, links, and other information in order to build brand and business awareness and your reputation as an expert. And of course it's similar to other networks in that your presence there will likely be a mixture of personal and professional updates.

But the biggest reason that it represents a 'must do' for your business is that Google made it a game-changer in terms of SEO (search engine optimization) and SEM (search engine marketing).

First off, your very presence on Google+ now impacts whether and where you turn up in Google search results. And it's not just being *on* Google+ that influences your visibility, it's also how Google+ perceives you as an influencer. The more followers you have and the more people who +1 your posts, the better you and your business will do in search results.

One more good reason to be on Google+ is that if you are on Facebook, LinkedIn and Google+ (and Twitter, for that matter) you can be happy about the fact that you are likely reaching different portions of your target markets on each, vs. feeling as though you are merely duplicating your efforts.

And this is another reason that you should target messages differently across these social media platforms, as well.

6. Pinterest (and other emerging platforms). The latest breakout on the social media scene is Pinterest. This network quietly made it's way into the top 10 social media networks in late 2011, coming pretty much out of nowhere to take the social media world by storm.

As a platform, it has some distinct advantages. Every "pin" has a component of visual appeal and by pinning and re-pinning the pins of other users, people self-identify their interests, tastes and loves. It provides users with the ability to talk about themselves and identify with products, brands, fashion, decor, quotes, food, lifestyles, art, architecture and a myriad of other visual representations.

As of this writing, businesses are just getting serious about Pinterest and learning how to use it to curate content relative to their products and services in ways that connect with users who may want to self-identify themselves with these same products and services.

Additionally, its also possible for users to use Pinterest to drive traffic for affiliate marketing, since when users click on a "pin" to find the original source, they are taken to outside websites including blogs, corporate websites and others.

And Pinterest's developers have provided the means for users to cross share pins to various other social platforms, thereby enabling users to simultaneously update Facebook and Twitter with visual "pins" for increased social media engagement but also to—again—self-identify themselves and their tastes and interests across multiple social media platforms.

7. Content Marketing Strategies. While not exclusive to social media, I wanted to include it here as a topic for consideration.

Apart from its SEO/SEM and other technical implications, ultimately, social media is about sharing content that is interesting and relevant to your members of the online communities where your customers are or which represent members of your target markets.

Your marketing plan must, therefore, address content marketing as a topic.

Essentially, content marketing includes both the creation of original content (on your website, your blog, on YouTube, on sites where your blog is syndicated or where you guest blog, etc.,) and content curation (which is when you round up content based on relevance to your customers and prospects for the purposes of sharing it with these audiences).

For instance, you can use an email newsletter both for content creation and curation, as I do. Each of my newsletters features link to original articles which I write on my blog, my website and on other blogs to which I contribute, and each of my newsletters also features links to the content of others which I believe will interest my readers.

This type of curation is important as it helps to build your reputation not only as an expert but as a valuable resource for your prospects and clients.

For those who still don't have a website

Some might be surprised to find that there are still business owners who don't think that they need a web presence. (I know I am.) (And I know you are out there because the absence of your presence on the w-w-w tells the story.)

In fact, there are many industries whose members have been particularly slow to come to the internet—small service-based businesses, independent restaurants, bars and boutiques and independent professionals, just to name a few.

But if you think about it, having an internet presence would be even more helpful for those types of businesses than it is for their larger competitors.

Why?

Because the internet makes it possible for you to compete with businesses of any size.

Because having a presence online ensures that you will receive at least *some* share of search traffic (**Hint:** if you don't have a website, the share of this traffic you receive is *none!*)

Because almost **80%** of U.S. consumers use the internet to find businesses online, locate brick and mortar locations, comparison shop and research products **prior to purchasing**.

Because, in fact, every month, **20%** of online searches are done by consumers looking for **local business resources**.

Because statistics show that even when individuals are attracted to a company through social media, that **before making a purchase, the vast majority still visit the corporate website** to find out more about a company or its products or services. (In other words, Facebook and other social media are essential business tools, but they do not replace a website!)

Because **more than half** of all Americans spend more than an hour online every day, and that statistic is even higher when it comes to professional men and women, moms, Baby Boomers, and increases yet again with individuals aged Gen X and younger.

In case I haven't been clear, the point is, your business needs a website of some kind. Period.

Your website can be as simple as a one page site that costs less than a hundred dollars a year (compare that with the cost of your yellow page listing!) with your contact information and one or two of the most compelling reasons people should book an appointment with you or visit your business. Or it can be a large, content-filled source of knowledge for consumers and employees. **What else can you do with your website?**

- Tell the story of your business, your core values, mission and vision.
- Tell people about the benefits of doing business with you. Educate consumers about the superiority of your products, services or organization.
- Tout the achievements and experience of employees.
- Make promises and guarantees.
- View your website as the means of establishing perceptions and setting expectations about your business and your brand in the clients mind.

Little White Marketing Lie #14:

"Bigger is better."

While most businesses waste valuable resources trying to become everything for everyone, niche marketing should be where you invest the majority of your marketing money and time.

Why? (I am always so glad you ask!)

Trying to be 'everything' to 'everyone' is not possible or desirable but it's a trap many businesses fall into.

In most cases, the result is bland and boring for everyone, including customers, prospects and staff.

Finding your niche is a two-dimensional project, and there is some "which came first, the chicken or the egg?" thinking to engage in.

Here is what I mean:

Inside: Part of finding your niche involves knowing 'who' you are: deciding how you will be unique and identifying characteristics and strengths that

> (1) set you apart from the competition and

> (2) are meaningful and attractive to prospects and customers.

Outside: The other aspect involves identifying both the types of clients your business, as defined above, is

> (1) likely to attract and

> (2) the types of people you actually want to attract, then creating strategies to do so.

Identifying the types of people your business is likely and those you most want to attract as customers gives you the ability to engage in target (or niche) marketing—and this is where you should receive the highest return on your marketing investment.

When you focus on niche marketing, you will do more, with less.

Why? Zeroing in on 'who' you want to attract gives you the ability to tailor messages specific enough to really get the attention of your target market.

And it also gives you the ability to put those tailored marketing messages directly in the path of your target market.

Take time to do your homework so you know the places where your ideal client types live, where else they shop, what they do for entertainment, where they go to school or church, what charities or community organizations they value, etc.

One of the most cost-effective ways to reach niche markets is to partner with other businesses, groups or organizations that share your target markets. You share costs and you expand outreach by sharing contacts.

In terms of other benefits, forming marketing partnerships with other organizations puts more resources, supplies, creativity, space and personnel at your disposal. You will have the ability to conduct larger campaigns, hold larger events and do more at those events—all of which means you will be that much more attractive to the very people you have decided are your prime niche markets. It's a win-win scenario, where you get both wins!

Little White Marketing Lie #15:

"When I apply my logo, I'm branding."

When thinking about the difference between self-improvement and building a better image, it struck me that in contrast to self-improvement, which often involves changes we make in order to feel better about ourselves, building a better image is about making improvements to change the way we appear to others or about making sure that we appear to others as we most desire to appear.

**This goes to the heart of branding.
And it has nothing to do with your logo.**

If you want a strong brand, you need to love your customers, not your logo.

Because your image (or brand) is really just that: perception. It's not your logo or business name, although those items are part of your brand's identity.

And so "branding" includes anything and everything you do in order to improve how customers and prospects think and feel about your business.

At its most basic and useful level, your brand image is the sum total of perceptions that exist in the customer's mind about who you are and the benefits of doing business with you that is established, and either reinforced or undermined, each and every time they come in contact with you or any facet of your business.

Building a better image is about putting the stamp of the personality, values, culture, beliefs—the very essence of everything you really want your business to be—on every possible customer touch point.

Why is this important?

Without a strong brand image, you have to build a case for why you deserve someone's business, every single time you get ready to make a sale.

Businesses with strong brands have customers making purchases and telling their friends about them, while those that don't are still trying to introduce themselves.

And key to any brand improvement or overhaul you want to make are authenticity and employee buy-in, from the top down.

Why?

While you can refine any of the components of your brand identity (your logo, mission and vision statements, tag line, décor, customer guarantees and assurances, and even your product and service mix) to their ideal best, if the reality of the customer experience doesn't line up with the promises you are making, that image will be shattered. And once lost, it's difficult to regain customer trust.

You cannot control people's perceptions, but you can thoughtfully design all of those elements of your brand identity which are under your control in order to build the best possible image in the mind of your customers and prospects. And that is really what branding is all about.

Need a starting point? Download a free branding checklist from the Resources page of my website at www.12monthsofmarketing.net.

I hope that you have been entertained and provoked (at least a little) by these Little White Marketing Lies. For more marketing resources or to read more of my articles or books, visit my website at www.12monthsofmarketing.net or my marketing blog at http://365daysofmarketingblog.blogspot.com.

It's going to be a great year!

Elizabeth Kraus

www.ingramcontent.com/pod-product-compliance
Lightning Source LLC
Chambersburg PA
CBHW081455170526
45166CB00008B/2435